Child Poverty and Deprivation in the UK

Child Poverty and Deprivation in the UK

by

Professor Jonathan Bradshaw
University of York

on behalf of the

NATIONAL CHILDREN'S BUREAU
for the United Nations Children's Fund

Published by the National Children's Bureau,
8 Wakley Street, London EC1V 7QE
Telephone 071-278 9441

© National Children's Bureau 1990

ISBN 0 902 817 57 4

Printed by Saxon Printing Ltd, Derby

All rights reserved. No part of this publication may be produced, stored in a retrieval system or transmitted in any form by any person without the written permission of the publisher.

The National Children's Bureau was established as a registered charity in 1963. Our purpose is to identify and promote the interests of all children and young people and to improve their status in a diverse and multiracial society.

We work closely with professionals and policy makers to improve the lives of all children but especially children under five, those affected by family instability and children with special needs or disabilities.

We collect and disseminate information about children and promote good practice in children's services through research, policy and practice development, publications, seminars, training and an extensive library and information service.

Contents

List of tables		vii
Preface		viii
1	Foreword	1
2	Introduction	3
3	Child poverty in historical perspective from the 1940s to the 1970s	6
4	Child poverty in the 1980s	10
5	Inequality in the 1980s	17
6	The causes of child poverty and deprivation in the 1980s	
	• Economic trends	19
	• Demographic changes	21
	• Policies:	22
	– Taxation	23
	– Social benefits	23
	– Services	25
	– Child Rights	29
7	The impact on children (Physical)	32
	• Infant mortality	33
	• Childhood deaths	35
	• Child morbidity	36
	• Child development	38
	• Racial disadvantage	40
	• Homelessness and housing conditions	40

- Clothing 42
- Child protection 43
- Child abuse 43

(Behavioural)
- Educational attainment 45
- Truancy 45
- Teenage conceptions 46
- Pocket money 46
- Child labour 47
- TV viewing 47
- Smoking 47
- Drinking 48
- Drugs 49
- Juvenile crime 50

8 Conclusions 51

References 53

Index 60

List of tables

1 Children in families with low incomes, 1979-1985 — 11
2 Persons in families living below 110 per cent of the SB level, 1979-1985 — 13
3 Percentage of dependent children living in households with income below 50 per cent of the average, income after housing costs, 1979-1987 — 14
4 Number of children in families receiving family income supplement and supplementary benefit, 1978-1988 — 15
5 Supplementary benefit/income support scales for a couple with two children aged under 11 a) at constant price, b) as a proportion of the median disposable income of a couple with two children — 16
6 Changes in quintile income shares, 1979-1987 — 18
7 Real increase in benefit rates following the introduction of income support — 25
8 Destinations of 16-18 year olds — 27
9 Infant mortality, vital statistics UK, 1961-89 — 33
10 Childhood deaths, England and Wales, 1971-88 — 36
11 Trends in the percentage of children with reported morbidity, 1974, 1983 and 1987 — 37
12 Number of homeless households involving children, 1981-88 — 41
13 Notifiable sexual offences and homicides of children under 16, 1984-88 — 44
14 School leavers - highest qualification by sex, 1975/76 and 1986/87 — 45
15 Rates of conceptions among teenagers in England and Wales 1977, 1986 and 1987 — 46

Preface

Over the last few years, the National Children's Bureau has been reassessing its priorities in the light of our own values and principles. As a result, we have identified child poverty and deprivation as an important theme for future work.

Therefore, we were delighted when UNICEF's International Child Development Centre invited us to undertake the UK part of their international study on child poverty and deprivation in industrialised countries. In accepting this commission, we realised that we would need to seek an expert outside the Bureau to research and write the report and I believe that the report we are now publishing illustrates how fortunate we were that Professor Jonathan Bradshaw agreed to be our author. His clearly written and very full survey of the difficult circumstances of the poorest and most deprived children in the UK today and the effects these circumstances have is a challenge to the National Children's Bureau and all those concerned with children's welfare.

The National Children's Bureau's work is always rooted in our knowledge base. One of the great strengths of Professor Bradshaw's report is the wealth of knowledge it brings together and the pointers it gives to areas where our knowledge is currently inadequate. We believe that this report must not be a once and for all publication and we are seeking to build on UNICEF's initiative by raising funds so that we can publish updated and extended reports at regular intervals. In this way, we can continue our tradition of providing policy makers and others with the basis for meeting the needs of children.

Barbara Kahan
Chair, National Children's Bureau

1. Foreword

This national case study on child poverty and deprivation in the UK was commissioned from the National Children's Bureau by the UNICEF International Child Development Centre based in Florence. It will contribute to an international comparative study of child poverty and deprivation in the industrialised countries.

In the past UNICEF has concentrated on the status of children in Third World countries and has produced, inter alia, its annual report *The State of the World's Children* (UNICEF: 1989). However, in the last 10-15 years there has been anxiety that improvements in the well-being of children in a number of industrialised countries has been slowing down and possibly even deteriorating. Furthermore

'...new and subtler forms of deprivation may have been caused by the profound changes occurring over the last forty years in labour markets, in environmental conditions, in family structure, in internal and international migration, in the organisation of society and in other aspects of life.' (UNICEF notes: May 1989)

UNICEF has therefore for the first time since its inception launched a study which will include a general review of the issues in all industrialised countries (about 30) and in depth analysis in eight countries, selected to represent different political, economic and social conditions. They are Hungary, Italy, Japan, Portugal, Sweden, UK, USA and the USSR.

My task was to review the position of children in the UK according to an analytical framework devised by Dr Andrea Cornia of UNICEF.

I am grateful for the help I have received in the scholarship involved in this task from Blair Howarth, Maeve Lobo and Liz

Allen, postgraduate students in my Department, and Nicola Hilliard, Head of the Library and Information Service at the National Children's Bureau. I am also grateful for the comments and encouragement I have received from Anne Weyman and David Berridge at the National Children's Bureau and Andrea Cornia at UNICEF.

I am not a specialist in every area of policy affecting children and this report has been 'validated' by others in the field including a specialist group of consultants convened by the National Children's Bureau. The section on child rights was drafted by Peter Smith.

The views expressed do not necessarily represent those of the National Children's Bureau or UNICEF.

Jonathan Bradshaw
University of York
September 1990

2. Introduction

The questions that UNICEF seeks to answer are very important. If the improvement in the well-being of children in the UK has slowed down or deteriorated in the last ten years then we ought to know about it. If, in the face of the profound changes that many countries have experienced, children have suffered in the UK more than elsewhere then it is a fundamental criticism of the way in which our society has responded to those changes. If we can identify ways in which the well-being of children has failed to make progress then it gives us targets to aim at in the 1990s and beyond. In any society, the state of children should be of primary concern – their well-being is not only an indication of a society's moral worth, they are human capital, the most important resource for its national future.

'.... children must come first because children are our most sacred trust. They also hold the key to our future in a very practical sense. It will be their ideas and their resourcefulness which will help solve such problems as disease, famine and the threats to the environment and it is their ideas and their values which will shape the future character and culture of our nation. We need to do all we can to ensure that children enjoy their childhood against a background of secure and loving family life. That way, they can develop their full potential, grow up into responsible adults and become, in their turn, good parents.' (Margaret Thatcher, George Thomas Society, Inaugural Lecture, 17 January 1990.)

Perhaps an ominous reflection of the position in the UK is that it is difficult to answer the questions that UNICEF has posed. The essence of the problem is that while the UK has what constitutes an excellent national data base on family or household living standards, social conditions and social attitudes, children have not been the primary focus of attention. Furthermore the investigation of children's progress requires investigation over time and although there is a rich variety of primary research and official statistics covering child poverty, deprivation, health and well being, it is often not population based, it is cross sectional in approach and does not allow the analysis of change over time. Even the three great birth cohort studies in the UK are of limited use for this purpose because although they can tell us what has happened to children born in 1949, 1958 and 1970 they cannot say how children of a given age in 1980 and children of the same age in 1990 compare.

UNICEF has quite rightly emphasised outputs and impacts rather than inputs. In considering children's well-being we should try to concentrate not on inputs such as the amounts of child benefit and other benefits or expenditure on services but on outputs such as the school enrolment rates or the availability of playgrounds and, more importantly, on impacts such as school performance, infant mortality or the heights and weights of children. There is, of course, generally much better data on inputs than there is on outputs and impacts.

In order to focus on policy, it is necessary to be able to relate inputs to impacts – to be able to conclude, for example, that a slowing down in the decline of the rate of infant mortality is related to increases in material deprivation or a deterioration in child health and maternity services. This and similar links between inputs and impacts are almost impossible to draw. Indeed in health there is a conceptual problem in that ill health can be the result of deprivation or it can lead to deprivation. What is needed is detailed international comparative research of the type that UNICEF aspires to. Meanwhile at a national level we often have to rely, where it is available, on evidence of differentials in the rate of change between groups in the UK.

The final problem we face in responding to UNICEF's commission is that much of the evidence that might be available on the impact on children of changes in the last 10–15 years is not yet available. This is partly due to the fact that the data has not yet emerged. Large scale nationally representative surveys take time to be analysed and published and, working in 1990, for many aspects of the subject the latest data still relates to the mid 1980s. More profoundly, the real consequences for children of increasing poverty, cuts in benefits and services and the impact of demographic changes have yet to be observed. The manner in which material, emotional and social processes have an impact on children, affect them in adolescence and influence their lives as adults, as parents, in employment and in old age are, to say the very least, not well understood. There is no doubt that human beings are robust. They learn to live with life. But children are also vulnerable and their vulnerability is why we should be concerned to seek to answer the questions posed by UNICEF, even if the answers are to some extent tentative and premature.

3. Child poverty in historical perspective from the 1940s to the 1970s

Britain emerged from the Second World War with a national consensus committed to the establishment of a 'welfare state' that would attack Beveridge's five giants: want, disease, ignorance, squalor and idleness. A spate of legislation in the 1940s led to the introduction of family allowances, national assistance, a national insurance scheme covering the major contingencies – unemployment, widowhood, sickness and retirement, a national health service free at the point of demand and a national education scheme for all children aged 5–15. At the same time economic policies based on Keynesian principles led to levels of employment unprecedented in the prewar world with a sharp increase in dual earner families. Between 1945 and 1980:

- real Gross Domestic Product increased by 139 per cent;
- real disposable incomes per head increased by 84 per cent (between 1954 and 1976);
- the average working hours of manual workers fell from 47 hours per week to 43 hours per week;
- most social security benefits more than doubled in real terms;
- for most of the period the level of unemployment remained below 600,000.

There is no doubt that this period for most British people was one of unprecedented improvement in living standards.

By the mid 1960s it was thought that full employment, redistributive fiscal and social policies and the institutions of the welfare state had eradicated poverty. However academic research began to reveal that our faith in the efficacy of full employment has been misguided, our analysis of the effects of tax and social policies inadequate and we only had a partial understanding of the impact of the welfare state. By conventional standards a substantial minority of the population were still living in poverty and also conventional standards were being criticised as inappropriate in a society with increasing affluence. Abel Smith and Townsend (1965) found 14 per cent of the population with incomes below 140 per cent of the assistance scale in 1960.

We do not have a series of figures that trace trends in poverty and inequality consistently over the last 45 years. Although there has always been a minority of families with children living on low incomes due to unemployment, low wages, disablement or lone parenthood, there is no doubt that with rising earnings and real increases in benefits if a series had existed up to 1979 it would show that the proportion in poverty had fallen and inequalities were certainly being reduced (Halsey: 1988).

Over the last 45 years the UK has experienced some quite sharp fluctuations in the birth rate. Following the end of the war the fertility rate began to rise, fell slightly in the early 1950s, then rose again reaching a peak in the early 1960s and from the early 1970s has remained below replacement level. The result of this fluctuation is that the total number of people aged 0-24 rose from 18.2 million in 1951 to 21.6 million in 1971 and in 1986 had fallen back to 20.1 million (see Chart 1).

Despite these fluctuations in the number of children the general improvement in living standards, the health and welfare services and changes in family characteristics all contributed to a rapid improvement in the status of children. Between 1949-1979 the infant mortality rate more than halved falling from 29.1 per 1000 to 13.1 per 1000. Over the same period the life expectancy of men and women improved by five years. Child death rates fell to a third of their level in 1946/50. Deaths from infectious diseases are now negligible compared with their rates in the prewar period (Halsey: 1988).

In most areas of public expenditure there were increases in real terms and as a proportion of GDP. In education the statutory school leaving age was increased to fifteen in 1947 and sixteen in 1973. Selectivity in education was abandoned in most areas and by the end of the 1970s nearly three-quarters of all children were attending comprehensive schools. Despite an increase in school rolls which peaked in 1974 in primary schools and 1977 in secondary schools, there has been a steady increase in the teacher pupil ratios. The

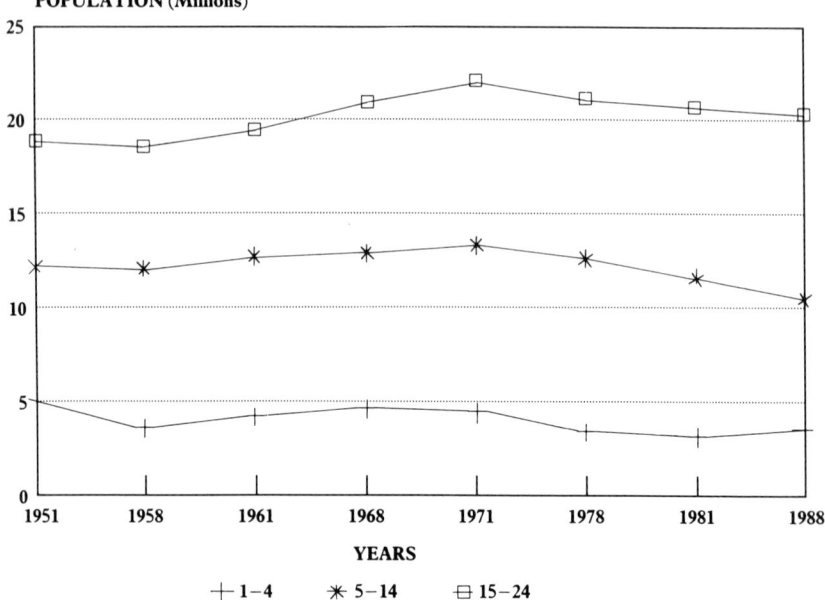

Chart 1: Population fluctuation 1951-1988

+ 1-4   ✲ 5-14   ▭ 15-24

proportion of children staying on after school leaving age also increased (Halsey: 1988).

During the period there were also substantial improvements in the size and condition in the housing stock with nearly 10 million new homes built between 1945–1979 in England and Wales and a massive slum clearance programme. There was a substantial fall in overcrowding, shared dwellings, unfit dwellings and dwellings lacking amenities. The tenure of the housing stock also shifted with the decline in ownership by private landlords from over a half to less than a sixth and the growth of owner occupation from less than a third to over a half (Halsey: 1988).

The 'Butskellite' consensus on the value of the welfare state began to break down from the mid 1960s. Critics from the left and the right began to point to its failure to abolish poverty, to the fact that despite high levels of taxation and public expenditure many social problems remained and some were getting worse. Critics from the left suggested that public expenditure was tending to benefit middle and upper income groups more than the poor (Le Grand: 1982). On the right there was a belief that public expenditure was too high and crowding out private consumption and investment; that high levels of taxation required to fund public services were restricting choice and freedom, reducing incentives to work and save, undermining enterprise and increasing dependency. It was thought that the institutions of the welfare state had become a self serving, inefficient bureaucracy and it was time to turn back to the traditional family, voluntary effort and private and occupational provision to meet need. These ideas found expression in the election of a Conservative Government led by Mrs Margaret Thatcher in 1979. What have been the consequences for children?

4. Child poverty in the 1980s

The notion of poverty in the UK is not uncontroversial. Unlike some other countries, Britain does not have a definition of poverty or a poverty level which is generally accepted. In June 1989 John Moore, then Secretary of State for Social Security, claimed the 'end of the line for poverty', that living standards had improved so much since the early part of the century and the prewar period, that poverty had no longer any real meaning and 'that individuals and organisations concerned with poverty were merely pursuing the political goal of equality'. (Speech text 11 May 1989)

While there is no agreement about the notion of poverty there is also heated debate about the validity of statistics on poverty. One government series which has been used to assess the prevalence of poverty is the *Statistics on Low Income Families*. These estimates were derived from the annual *Family Expenditure Survey*, and produced annually from 1974 until 1979 and then biennially until 1985 when the series was suspended by the Government. The advantages of the statistics were that they related the income of families to the national scales of benefit paid as social assistance (supplementary benefit) to those out of employment. This is effectively the minimum safety-net that Parliament and Government have decided people should live on if they have no other resources. It is also an 'equivalent' standard that takes account of variations in family composition and has its origin in the minimum subsistence budgets devised to represent poverty in the prewar era.

It can be seen in Table 1 that the number of children living in families with incomes around the supplementary benefit (SB) standard increased between 1979 and 1985 by 49 per cent. By 1985, 3.5 million children or 28.6 per cent of all children were living

CHILD POVERTY IN THE 1980s

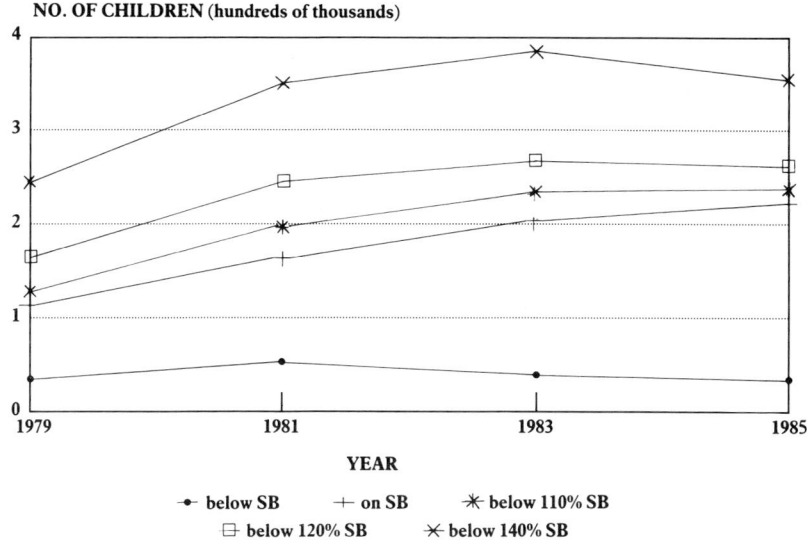

Chart 2: Children in low income families
Families below 140% of the SB level

– below SB + on SB ✶ below 110% SB
□ below 120% SB ✕ below 140% SB

Table 1: Children in families with low incomes – Thousands

	1979	1981	1983	1985	% change 1979–85
Income below SB level	300	530	400	360	+ 20
Receiving SB	880	1160	1630	1890	+115
Income above SB level but below 110% of SB	150	280	310	190	+ 27
Income above 110% of SB level but below 120% of SB	290	390	370	210	− 28
Income above 120% of SB level but below 140% of SB	760	1220	1170	900	+ 18
ALL	2380	3580	3880	3550	+ 49
% of all children	17.9	27.4	30.8	28.6	+ 60

Source: Derived from DSS Social Security Statistics

around this standard. Chart 2 shows how the number of children in families with low incomes has fluctuated over that period.

There are two principal criticisms of this standard:

- The justification for taking a higher standard than the actual supplementary benefit scales as the poverty standard is that families dependent on supplementary benefit have as a result of disregarded earnings and savings and additional payments, incomes rather above the 100 per cent level. However to use a standard which incorporates about a third of the population as living in poverty and on the margin of poverty does not appear to be intuitively right and so in Table 2, below the 110 per cent level is taken as the income standard.
- If supplementary benefit levels are improved in real terms (that is, faster than the rate of inflation) then it has the paradoxical effect of increasing the numbers of people defined as poor. The level of the scale rates of benefit have in fact more than doubled in real terms since they were introduced in 1948. However between 1979 and 1985 they only increased by 5.8 per cent in real terms (Department of Social Security (DSS): 1989) and the Government estimates that only 45 per cent of the increase in the numbers living below the 110 per cent of SB level between 1979 and 1985 was the result of the real increase in the SB scales. (Hansard 1 May 1990 col.491.)

However there is a justification for increasing the poverty standard over time – in order to maintain parity with improvements in earnings. In fact the value of benefits in relation to earnings, despite improvements in real terms, is lower now than it was in 1948 and the level of benefit as a percentage of average male earnings fell by 8.1 per cent between 1979 and 1985 (DSS: 1989). This means that families with incomes at or around SB level lost ground in comparison with those with incomes from work. Indeed the gap between the incomes of the employed and the unemployed is wider than that represented by average male earnings because there has also been an increase in dual earner families among the employed. Between 1979 and 1988 the SB scale rates for a couple with one child aged 5–10 as a proportion of mean normal weekly disposable income, has fallen from 32 per cent to 25 per cent (see also Table 5).

Table 2 and Chart 2 take the 110 per cent level as the poverty standard and show that the number of persons in poverty between 1979 and 1985 increased by 111 per cent. Families with children living in poverty can be divided into four groups: families with a head

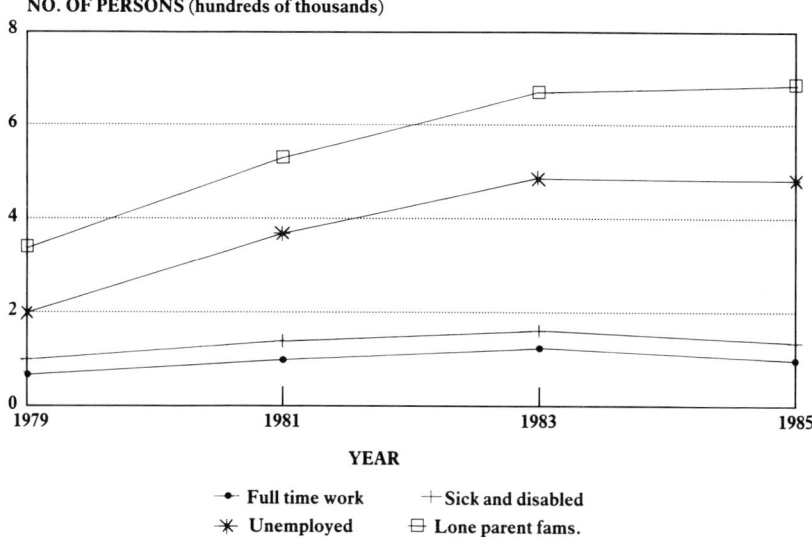

Chart 3: Persons in low income families
Families below 110% of the SB level

→ Full time work   + Sick and disabled
※ Unemployed   ⊟ Lone parent fams.

Table 2: Persons in families living below 110 per cent of the SB level. Thousands

	1979	1981	1983	1985	% change 1979–85
Head of family in full time employment	700	1040	1220	930	33
Sick/disabled	300	390	380	380	27
Unemployed	1040	2290	3310	3560	242
Other (including lone parent families)	1300	1530	1950	2170	67
ALL	3340	5250	6860	7040	111
% of all persons	7.5	11.8	15.3	15.6	(108)

Source: DSS Social Security Statistics

in full time work, lone parent families, families with an unemployed head and families where the head is sick or disabled. All these groups have increased in size during the 1980s. It will be seen later how this has occurred.

Unfortunately, despite criticism of the decision from a number of bodies including the Social Services Committee of the House of Commons (Social Services Committee 1988a), the *Low Income Families* statistical series was not continued beyond 1985. The Institute of Fiscal Studies has however produced *Low Income Families* tables for 1985 and 1987. Unfortunately they were unable to reconcile their 1985 figures with the official estimates, so that 1987 figures are not comparable with those in the table above. However between 1985 and 1987 their figures show that the number of children living in families with incomes below 140 per cent of SB again rose by 50,000 and the number of persons in families with incomes below 110 per cent of SB increased by 600,000 (IFS: 1990).

The Low Income Families tables have been replaced with a new series giving the proportion of 'Households Below Average Income'. The new series has so far only been published for the period 1979 to 1987 and so it is not possible to use it to trace changes in the proportion of children in families with low incomes over the decade.

Table 3 presents the change in the proportion of dependent children living in households with incomes below 50 per cent of the average. It shows that between 1979 and 1987, the proportion of children living below 50 per cent of average income more than doubled from 12.2 per cent to 25.7 per cent. There were fluctuations

Table 3: Percentage of dependent children living in households with incomes below 50 per cent of the average, income after housing costs 1979–1987

	1979	1981	1983	1985	1987
Children in households of:					
Full time workers	5	8	6	6	13
Single parents	45	42	29	35	60
Unemployed	69	78	76	88	79
Pensioners, sick and others	40	31	38	37	46
ALL	12.2	18.0	16.6	19.8	25.7

Source: Table F3 Households Below Average Incomes: DSS

from year to year but over the period the proportion increased whatever the economic status of the family head. In the absence of a series covering poverty over the whole decade, administrative statistics on the number of children receiving various benefits also provide a proxy for the number of children living on low incomes. Table 4 presents the number of children dependent on supplementary benefit because their parents are sick, disabled, unemployed or lone parents and on family income supplement because their parents have low earnings, from 1978-1988. It shows that the number of children living in families dependent on these benefits has more then doubled in the last decade. Although it is estimated that 30 per cent of the increased numbers on SB (between 1979 and 1985) is due to improvements in the real level of benefits there is no doubt that more children are living in families dependent on basic benefits.

Table 4: Number of children in families receiving family income supplement and supplementary benefit 1978–1988. Thousands.

	FIS	S B	of whom unemployed	ALL
1978	185	1036	NA	1221
1979	184	918	339	1102
1980	NA	1084	494	NA
1981	222	1485	810	1707
1982	306	1711	948	2017
1983	396	1781	977	2177
1984	417	1938	1053	2355
1985	405	NA	NA	NA
1986	405	2113	1087	2518
1987	446	2100	965	2546
1988	428	2104	NA	2532

Source: DSS Social Security Statistics. NA = Not available.

Because of the importance of supplementary benefit to the living standards of low income families and to the definition of poverty in the UK, it is worth being aware of what has happened to the real level of the benefit over time. Table 5 shows that between 1978 and 1989 the real level of benefits has increased by £8.58 (11 per cent) but because earnings have risen faster than prices, as a proportion of net disposable income it has fallen by nearly a fifth from 37 per cent to 30 per cent.

Table 5: Supplementary benefit/income support scales for a couple with two children aged under 11 (a) at constant prices (b) as a proportion of the median disposable income of a couple with two children.

	In real April 1989 terms £ per week	As % median disposable income of a couple with two children
1978	79.82	37.4
1979	80.05	37.0
1980	80.63	36.5
1981	77.79	36.2
1982	81.36	37.0
1983	81.50	35.9
1984	81.37	35.5
1985	81.80	34.2
1986	80.50	31.3
1987	78.73	30.2
1988	81.83	NA
1989	88.40	NA

What does it mean to live on incomes at or around supplementary benefit level income in the UK? One recent study (Bradshaw and Holmes: 1989) of a sample of families with children with an unemployed head living on supplementary benefit in the north east of England concluded

> 'The picture which emerges from this detailed study of family lives is one of constant restriction in almost every aspect of people's activities.... The lives of these families, and perhaps most seriously the lives of the children in them, are marked by the unrelieved struggle to manage with dreary diets and drab clothing.
>
> 'They also suffer what amounts to cultural imprisonment in their homes in our society in which getting out with money to spend on recreation and leisure is normal at every other income level.' pp.138–139.

5. Inequality in the 1980s

Data on the distribution of incomes during the 1980s is also not up to date and not easy to interpret but there is growing evidence that during the decade, post war trends towards greater equality in the distribution of income and wealth came to a halt and have been reversed. Table 6 is based on the annual analysis carried out by the Central Statistical Office and published in *Economic Trends*. It compares the distribution of shares of original income (income from earnings, rents, dividends and interest) and shares of final income (after the impact of social security benefits, direct and indirect taxation and the benefits of housing, health and education expenditure and transport subsidies) between 1979 and 1987. It shows that the share of original income of the bottom two quintiles has fallen from 9.5 per cent to 6.3 per cent and that of the top quintile has risen from 45 per cent to 51 per cent. Between 1979 and 1987 the share of final income of the bottom 20 per cent fell by 11 per cent and that of the top 20 per cent rose by 11 per cent. Gini coefficients (measures of inequality) on both original and final income have increased indicating an increase in inequality.

There is evidence (Economic Trends: 1988) that families with children have been particularly affected by this increase in income inequalities. In 1979, nine per cent of the bottom quintile group of original income consisted of families with children. By 1986 this proportion had increased to 19 per cent (see also Roll: 1988).

Johnson and Stark (1989) have used a model of the UK population and simulated the effects of tax and social security changes between 1979 and 1989, to assess their impact on income distribution. Their analysis is defective in that it assumes full take-up of income tested benefits but they conclude that there was an increase in average real

Table 6: Changes in quintile income shares 1979–1987

		Quintile group					Gini coefficient
		Lowest 1st	2nd	3rd	4th	Highest 5th	
Original income							
	1979	0.5	9	19	27	45	45
	1987	0.3	6	16	27	51	52
Final income							
	1979	7.1	12	18	24	38	32
	1987	6.3	11	17	24	42	36

Source: Economic Trends, May 1990

income for all households of £7 per week. However the rich and the working population did much better than the poor and the non-working population. Whereas the richest decile gained an average of £30 per week the poorest decile gained only £2 per week. Families with children gained on average but not nearly as much as single and two earner couples without children. Thus there has been a growth in both vertical and horizontal inequality over the last ten years.

6. The causes of child poverty and deprivation in the 1980s

Three interacting factors have contributed to the increase in the prevalence of child poverty and deprivation in the UK in the 1980s: economic trends, demographic changes and social policies. They will be discussed in turn.

Economic trends

The economy of the UK had been suffering from endemic long term weaknesses for many years even before the 1980s. These were characterised by low levels of investment, low levels of productivity, high levels of trade disputes, higher levels of inflation than its competitors', a trade imbalance and low levels of economic growth. However the economic factor that had most impact on children in the 1980s has been the high level of unemployment, unprecedented in the post war era. The level of unemployment was certainly exacerbated by the Government's supply side determination to give priority to controlling inflation. The annual rate of inflation had reached 24 per cent in 1975. The workforce in employment fell rapidly between 1979 and 1983 and unemployment increased from 1.4 million in 1979 to 3.7 million in 1985 and 1986. Although labour demand began to pick up after 1983, unemployment has continued at very high levels. This was due to an increase in labour supply caused by an increase in the number of young people entering the labour market as a result of earlier birth bulges in the 1960s and an increase in the labour supply of married women. (By 1987, 60 per cent of married women with children were in employment, including 46 per cent of those with children aged 3-4 [11 per cent full time and 35 per cent part time]). As a result unemployment only began to fall in 1986 when labour demand continued to grow and because the supply of young people entering the labour force declined.

Over the decade 27 changes were made to the unemployment statistics which resulted in a reduction in the official unemployment numbers. If these changes are ignored, by May 1990, 2.5 million people were still unemployed (Unemployment Unit: 1990).

During the 1980s long term unemployment also increased: in October 1981, only 26 per cent had been unemployed for over one year but by October 1989 that proportion had risen to 38 per cent (Department of Employment (DOE): 1989). The policies which exacerbated unemployment had an impact on the rate of inflation, which fell from an annual rate of 18 per cent in 1980 to 3.4 per cent in 1986. They also arguably led to other economic improvements including an increase in productivity and economic growth. But these improvements were achieved at great social costs and furthermore the benefits may be short lived. At the end of the decade inflation has risen again to 10 per cent, interest rates are at record post war levels, the balance of trade deficit is higher than it was in 1979, the rate of economic growth is slowing down (Treasury: 1989) and unemployment began to rise again in April 1990.

The other important factor that affected the living standards of families during the 1980s concerns what has happened to earnings. Differentials in earnings have increased in the 1980s. Salaries have increased faster than wages, the wages of skilled workers faster than unskilled and differentials between the earnings of men and women, which began to narrow following equal pay legislation in the 1970s, have since 1981 remained stable with women's earnings at 67 per cent of men's. The earnings of young people have also fallen further behind those of adults: between 1979 and 1989, young people's earnings as a proportion of adult earnings fell from 61 per cent to 54 per cent for 18–20-year-olds and from 42 per cent to 39 per cent for 16–17-year-olds (Low Pay Unit: 1990). There is no minimum wage in Britain and low pay is endemic and has increased. Wages councils which exist to protect the low paid have been undermined by understaffing and wages council protection for the young people was abolished in 1986. A survey in Manchester in 1989 revealed that 76 per cent of jobs advertised in job centres for young people were paying less than the rate that would have applied under wages council protection (Low Pay Unit: 1990). Between 1979 and 1988, the number of wage earners falling below the Council of Europe's 'decency threshold' increased from 7.8 million to 9.9 million (Low Pay Unit: 1989).

Demographic changes

During the 1980s there have been some significant changes in family structure which have affected the prevalence of child poverty. In common with other European countries, UK fertility rates have been below replacement level since the early 1970s and the UK population under 16 has fallen from 13.7 million in 1976 to 11.5 million in 1988. The reasons for this decline in fertility are not fully understood. It is possible that much of it is caused by the use of birth control measures and abortion (abortions in England and Wales increased from 109,000 in 1976 to 180,000 in 1988 [*Social Trends*: 1990]) to delay child bearing. However it is also probable that the increased labour participation of married women has increased the direct and indirect costs of child rearing quite apart from the profound changes in their attitudes, aspirations and beliefs about gender roles.

During the 1980s relationships between men and women have also become more fragile, tentative and insecure as a base for child rearing. Until 1971, marriage had never been more popular but it now appears to be declining. The rate of first marriages per 1,000 unmarried population over 16 (in Great Britain) declined from 68.5 in 1971 to 42.1 in 1988. Also the remarriage rate of divorced persons, which had also been rising until the mid 1970s, has since decreased from 134 per thousand divorced women (England and Wales) in 1976 to 66.6 in 1988. Cohabitation before marriage, between marriages and as an alternative to marriage has been increasing rapidly and the length of cohabitation has been increasing. The proportion of single women cohabiting increased from 8 per cent in 1981 to 17 per cent in 1987. The proportion of women who had experienced cohabitation before marriage increased from about 20 per cent of marriages in 1975 to 53 per cent of marriages in 1987. In 1986/87 there were about 400,000 children living with cohabiting couples (Haskey and Kiernan: 1989). Divorce increased sharply in 1971 when the Divorce Reform Act 1969 became operative. The divorce rate rose steadily after that and appeared to peak at 12.9 per thousand married people in 1985. It is estimated that one in three new marriages will end in divorce and the chances of divorce are higher for second marriages, younger marriage and marriages following cohabitation (Wicks: 1989).

One result of this decline in marriage, is more children are being reared in lone parent families (Haskey: 1989). In 1986 there were over a million lone parent families and 14 per cent of all families with children are lone parent families, 90 per cent of them headed by a female. About 1.6 million children now live with a lone parent and it is estimated that a third of all children will experience living in a lone parent family (Clarke: 1989).

There has been a rapid increase in the proportion of children born outside wedlock in the 1980s – from 9.2 per cent in 1976 to 27 per cent in 1989. This is a much higher rate than most industrialised countries. However it is estimated that two thirds of these births are registered by both parents and 70 per cent are at the same address and, thus, may be stably cohabiting. The number of single lone parents has been increasing, however they still only represent 26 per cent of the total – 66 per cent of lone mothers are separated or divorced and 9 per cent are widowed.

Divorce and remarriage has led to an increasing diversity of family life in the last ten years and an increasing proportion of children are having to adjust to living with their natural mother and a stepfather. It is estimated that by 2000 only half of all children will spend their childhood with both natural parents (Kiernan and Wicks: 1990). There is dispute in the literature on the impact of these changes in family structure on the well-being of children – whether the life chances of children from lone parent families are disadvantaged in comparison with being brought up in a two parent household. However there is no doubt that the incidence of poverty is much greater in lone parent families (Millar: 1989). Maintenance (alimony) from former partners is received by less than a third of lone parents and payments are low and irregular. At a time when the labour participation rates of married women have been increasing, the proportion of lone mothers in work has declined and during the 1980s the proportion of lone parents dependent on social security has increased.

Policies

During the whole of the 1980s social and fiscal policies have been in the hands of a Government committed to reductions in taxation and public expenditure. However despite these commitments, public expenditure has risen in real terms by around 11 per cent a year since

1979. Public expenditure as a proportion of GNP was 43·25 per cent in 1978/79, rose to 46·75 per cent in 1982/83 and was still 43·5 per cent in 1986/87. Since then it has fallen as a proportion of GNP to 39 per cent in 1990/91, but this is the result of the economy growing as well as expenditure cuts.

The reason for this failure to achieve the cuts in public expenditure intended are complex and fascinating – they are certainly partly due to the massive costs of providing benefits for the unemployed, prematurely retired and the sick and disabled, partly the demands of an ageing population and partly the high level of support among the general public for welfare state spending, which has tended to increase over the decade. However what is important for this report is to describe what has happened to the taxes, benefits and services that affect children.

Taxation Since 1979 the tax system has become vertically more regressive and remains horizontally neutral. (The latter because children are no longer recognised in the tax system.) There has been a shift from direct taxation of income and capital to indirect taxation of consumption. Rates of income tax have been cut, particularly for higher rate payers. Cuts in income tax have been partly offset by increases in national insurance contributions. Personal tax allowances have been increased at a faster rate than price inflation but have not kept pace with increases in earnings. The consequences of these changes are that the proportion of higher incomes taken in tax has fallen while that of lower incomes has risen (Hill: 1989).

Social benefits The major change in social security during the 1980s was the decision of the Government to break the link between the level of benefits and earnings. Since 1980, the main benefits have been uprated in line with prices (see Table 5). Thus the living standards of those dependent on social security benefits relative to those in work have declined as earnings have moved ahead of prices. A second change has occurred as a result of a shift from contributory and universal benefits to selective income related benefits. These means-tested benefits are not claimed by many of those entitled to them and create inequities and possibly disincentives in combination with the tax system when they are withdrawn as incomes rise. The most significant victim of this policy has been child benefit: the level of child benefit, which has not been generous in the European context (Bradshaw and Piachaud: 1980) has been frozen for the past three years and a means tested benefit for low wage families (family credit) has been enhanced, though to date it is only being claimed by about half of those thought to be eligible. The consequence of the freezing of child benefit is that those families not receiving family credit are worse off than they would be otherwise. Child benefit has been paid at the rate of £7.25 per child per week since April 1987. If it had been uprated since then in line with inflation it would be worth £8.60 in April 1990.

The social security system has undergone a number of incremental changes since 1979. Apart from those already mentioned, the most significant for children have been the cumulative effects of the changes in benefits for the unemployed and the impact of the reform replacing supplementary benefit with income support and reducing the role of housing benefit. Since 1979, there have been a series of often small technical changes to benefits for the unemployed, either motivated by a desire to reduce the costs of benefits or to increase work incentives. Among these has been the abolition of child addition to short term insurance benefits and child support for those on unemployment benefit has declined by a third in real terms between 1978 and 1989 (Hansard 6 November 1989). Atkinson (1989) has carried out a systematic analysis of the cumulative affects of the changes in benefits for the unemployed between 1979 and 1988 and calculated that they add up to savings of £465 million and unemployed claimants are £2.92 per week worse off as a result.

As we have seen in Table 4 there has been a large increase in the number of people dependent on the basic assistance benefit (now called income support) during the 1980s. In fact one person in seven in the UK is now dependent for all or part of their income on this one benefit. The principal reasons for the growth in the numbers on income support have been the high level of unemployment and the increase in the number of lone parent families. Unemployment benefit based on contributions only lasts a year and with so many of the unemployed having exhausted their entitlement or never having built up an entitlement through insurance contributions, three quarters of the unemployed including a million children have become dependent on income support. As we have seen, the number of lone parent families has grown rapidly, so has their dependence on benefits. At a time when an increasing proportion of married women have entered the labour force, the proportion of lone parents in work has declined. Nearly three quarters of all lone parents including over a million children now depend on basic assistance income.

Thus over two million children have become dependent on income support and there has been anxiety that the level of benefit, especially for families with children, is not adequate. This was recognised by the Government in its intention to concentrate extra help on families with children in its 1986 White Paper on social security reform. It is not at all certain that this objective was achieved in practice and certainly no attempt was made to define adequacy. There were only modest changes in the structure and level of benefits following the reforms – (on the grounds that they were to be achieved at nil cost). Table 7 summarises the impact.

Table 7: Real increase in benefit rates following the introduction of income support (£ per week).

Lone parent plus a child aged 3	− £2.52
Lone parent plus children aged 4 and 6	− £2.56
Couple plus child aged 3	+ £0.72
Couple plus children aged 4 and 6	+ £0.68
Couple plus children aged 13 and 16	+ £2.91
Couple plus children aged 3, 8 and 11	+ £0.60
Couple plus children aged 6, 8, 11 and 16	+ £2.83

Source: Social Services Committee (HC 437–1 para.32 1989a)

Lone parents were worse off as a result of the introduction of income support and although couples with children gained in cash terms, their gains were modest and did not compensate on average for the fact that they had to pay 20 per cent of their rates and for the loss of extra (single) payments. These latter had been available under SB but were replaced by a, largely, loan based social fund under income support. As a result of the social security changes young people aged 16 and 17 have lost entitlement to income support altogether. In the last three annual upratings of benefits and in the context of the freezing of child benefit, the Government has provided small extra increases to the scale rates paid for children. However in 1990 an unemployed couple with two children aged 4 and 6 are entitled to only £89.65 per week and still have to pay their water rates and 20 per cent of their community charge (local tax paid by each adult in a household).

Services The impact of the Government's fiscal and public expenditure policies on services for children are more difficult to establish. They certainly vary from one sector to another and there is an interaction between the impact of benefit changes and demands on services.

Housing has suffered the sharpest cuts of all social expenditure – falling from 8 per cent of public expenditure in 1978/79 to 3.8 per cent in 1990/91. Expenditure (in 1986/87 real terms) has fallen from £7 billion in 1978/79 to £2.7 billion in 1989. This has resulted in a considerable fall in new house building in the public sector and a deterioration in the condition of the housing stock. Rents have also increased at a faster rate than general inflation and there has been a cyclical but significant increase in real house prices. This, coupled with high interest rates (despite a massive subsidy from tax relief on mortgage interest payments), has led to an increase in rent arrears, mortgage debt and repossession. The most dramatic result of these policies has been the increase in homelessness which as we shall see has exposed the lives of thousands more children to severe deprivation.

Education Public expenditure on education services has (in 1986/87 real terms) risen from £15.1 billion in 1978/79 to £16.5 billion in 1988/89 but educational expenditure as a proportion of total expenditure has fallen from 14.4 per cent in 1979 to 13.7 per cent in 1990/91. The total number of school pupils rose between 1961 and 1976 but between 1976 and 1987 it has fallen by 1.9 million.

- Pre-school provision: Provision for children under 5 (the statutory age of entry to full time education in the UK) falls into two different categories; nursery education in schools or nursery classes which is generally free and day care which almost invariably has to be paid for by parents. There are striking regional variations between the availability of types of provision. For example, of three-year-olds, 61.5 per cent in the north as opposed to 12.2 per cent in the south west receive nursery education (*Regional Trends*: 1990). The number of under fives in full time nursery education has remained constant. There has however been growth in the numbers attending part time nursery education, particularly in primary schools, from 117,000 in 1976 to 243,000 in 1988. Despite this, still less than half the children in the UK aged three and four are in pre-school education and most of this is part-time. The proportion of UK three and four-year-olds in pre-school education is particularly low when compared with other European countries (National Childcare Campaign/Day Care Trust: 1984).

Associated with rising rates of labour participation by married women there has been a significant increase in day care mostly provided by childminders (despite anxiety about some of its quality). Overall there has been an increase in the proportion of children under five in some form of day care from 14 per cent in 1976 to 20.1 per cent in 1988 (*Social Trends*: 1990).

• Primary, secondary and tertiary education: Thanks mainly to demographic changes class sizes have fallen slightly between 1979 and 1989 for both primary and secondary schools. The average class size in primary schools fell from 23.1 to 22.0 and in secondary schools from 16.7 to 15.3 (Hansard 20 March 1990, col.518).

The proportion of children staying on after statutory school leaving age has risen from 40 per cent in 1976 to 45 per cent in 1987 (although it is still low in comparison with other countries [*Social Trends*: 1990, Table 3.17]). But the proportion of children aged 16-18 in full time education rose only from 28 per cent to 32 per cent between 1976 and 1988. Table 8 shows that the education system failed to respond to increasing youth unemployment by increasing its provision of education and training.

Table 8: Destinations of 16–18-year-olds. Percentages

	1976	1981	1986	1987	1988
In full time education school	16	16	17	17	17
Further education	9	11	11	11	15
Higher education	3	3	3	3	
In employment	66	53	43	43	42
On Youth Employment Schemes	–	5	10	12	16
Unemployed	7	13	15	14	10

Source: Employment Gazette

In 1974 three per cent of 16–18-year-olds were unemployed, by 1981, 13 per cent were unemployed and five per cent in youth employment schemes. By 1988 the proportion unemployed had fallen back to 10 per cent, partly as a result of the extension of the Youth Training Scheme to two years' duration in 1987. The number of first degrees awarded has increased by about 40 per cent between 1979 and 1990.

The constraints on education expenditure have varied in their impact from area to area. Resources have been squeezed in some aspects of education more than others. The school meals service has deteriorated in the 1980s – largely because of the abolition of price maintenance and the nutritional standard of school meals. Average prices for a primary school meal have risen from 25p in 1979 to 65p in 1988. Four local authorities no longer provide paid meals and offer sandwiches to children entitled to free dinners. Between 1979 and 1988 the proportion of primary children in England taking a meal at school declined from 64 per cent to 43 per cent and between 1987 and 1988 there was a 31 per cent decline in the number of children taking free school meals (Child Poverty Action Group (CPAG): 1989). The proportion of children receiving free school meals was 14.7 per cent in 1978. It reached a peak of 19.8 per cent in 1986 and fell back to 11 per cent in 1989 (Hansard: 22 May 1990 col.98). The tertiary sector has also been squeezed with cuts in student grants, by 13 per cent, between 1978/79 and 1987/88. The earnings of teaching staff in schools and universities have also been held down with consequences for morale and more recently problems in teacher supply. Thousands of children in poorer inner city areas are unable to go to school because of the difficulty in recruiting staff. Expenditure per pupil in real terms on school books and equipment fell by 0.8 per cent for primary schools and 24.2 per cent for secondary schools between 1978/79 and 1987/88 (Hansard: 8 May 1989). Capital spending fell by 27 per cent between 1981 and 1988.

Health and Personal Social Services Overall expenditure on health has risen in real terms and as a proportion of GNP but there has been a lively debate about whether this growth in expenditure has been sufficient to meet the additional needs of an ageing population and advances in medical technology (Social Services Committee: 1989b). Attempts to redistribute health resources to underfunded regions and control health expenditure generally have led to painful problems of adjustment, with hospitals and wards having to be closed. Hospital waiting lists have fluctuated but by 1987 were 100,000 larger than they had been in 1976 – despite the fact that the throughput of patients in NHS hospitals increased by 26 per cent between 1971 and 1987.

It is not possible to assess how the maternity, child health and welfare services have fared in the competition for resources within the health and personal social services. Pre-natal diagnosis of congenital abnormalities and the abortion of damaged foetuses have led to a sharp decline in births of some disabled children but this has been offset by advances in surgical and medical interventions which have enabled more damaged children to remain alive longer. Over the decade there has been a continued gradual increase in the proportion of children vaccinated against the major childhood illnesses. However in 1987 the following proportion of children had still not been vaccinated – diphtheria 13 per cent, whooping cough 27 per cent, polio 13 per cent, tetanus 13 per cent, measles 24 per cent and rubella (girls only) 14 per cent. There are still also considerable regional differences in immunisation rates.

Policies to transfer mentally handicapped and mentally ill people from long stay institutions to care in smaller units in the community have reduced the already small proportion of children with mental handicaps in those institutions. New legislation has enhanced the rights of children with learning difficulties and the obligation of local authorities to protect their interests and plan for their future. Policies governing the protection of children have been reformed and re-reformed in the search for a balance between the rights of parents and the interests of children. There has been a steady decrease in the number and rate of children in the care of local authorities, but the total number of children removed by local authorities to a place of safety increased by 37 per cent between 1977 and 1987.

Child Rights The period under review from a children's rights perspective started auspiciously with the International Year of the Child in 1979 and ended with the passing of the Children Act 1989, which was heralded as the most comprehensive and far reaching reform of child law this century. At first sight a decade of progress could be deduced but the 1980s was a rather patchy and uneven decade for children's rights.

Freeman (1987–88) emphasises that 'rights without services are meaningless'. Heavy demands on limited resources for children's services have rendered ineffective some of the rights which children should enjoy. However, progress has been made in challenging the view of children as the property of their parents and increasing the requirements for children to be consulted about decisions concerning their future. The Children Act 1989 widens the circumstances in which courts and local authorities must find out the wishes and feelings of children and give them due consideration.

Guardians ad litem, who represent children's views to the court in care proceedings, were introduced in 1984 and will be more widely used under the Children Act. The Children Act 1989 allows children themselves to apply for a court order, for example to determine with whom they should live, or with whom they should have contact. Children's participation in criminal court proceedings as a witness has eased as procedures are beginning to be adopted that are more sensitive to children.

1989 was also an important year as it marked the adoption of the UN Convention on the Rights of the Child, which the British Government has expressed a general intention to ratify.

The celebrated Gillick case was potentially most significant in advancing children's rights because it established the principle that a child, given sufficient maturity and understanding, could have confidential medical and contraceptive advice against the wishes of a parent (Gillick v West Norfolk and Wisbech Area Health Authority [1986]1 FLR, No. 1, p 224). The Children Act 1989 extends the principle of a mature child having rights over his or her own medical treatment by enshrining in statute law the child's right, given sufficient age and understanding, to withhold consent to medical examination.

In education practice there have been some moves to encourage greater involvement of students in decision making regarding their schooling, in particular in allowing students greater choice of subjects, and greater participation in their own assessments. However, in law, there has been a shift away from student involvement in running schools. The 1986 Education (No. 2) Act outlawed student governors and gave greater powers to parent governors. It is feared that the Education Reform Act 1988, by imposing a National Curriculum, may reduce the student's ability to select areas of work. The predominant theme of the late 1980s has been parent choice in education on behalf of the child and this has almost eclipsed debate on student choice and student involvement.

The principle of parental responsibility is becoming more popular in Government pronouncements. Parental responsibility emphasises the duties and obligations parents have towards their children – a caring approach which few would decry. But the application of the principle in different policy areas encroaches on children's right to be seen as independent from parents and absolves the state of responsibility for children, which is shifted onto parents. For example, the cuts in real terms in student grants make more young people dependent on parents for longer; and most significantly, for hundreds of thousands of young people in Britain, their independent right to social security benefits has been reduced or abolished altogether. Not until the age of 25 do young adults receive the 'adult' rate of benefit.

7. The impact on children

Having reviewed the evidence of trends in poverty and inequality and the economic, demographic and social policies that may have had an affect on children's well-being in the 1980s, we now turn to review evidence of their impact on children. As has already been argued this is not a straight forward task: the data is often not available over time, is not up to date or has not yet been published. Many of the possible impacts may be long term and the consequences of the last 10 years for children's well-being are too early to assess. Indications of outcome can be considered under two broad headings.

- **Physical** which include
    - Infant mortality
    - Childhood deaths
    - Child morbidity
    - Child development
        Height
        Weight
        Nutrition
    - Racial disadvantage
    - Homelessness and housing conditions
    - Clothing
    - Child protection
    - Child abuse

- **Behavioural** which include
    - Educational attainment
    - Truancy
    - Teenage conceptions
    - Pocket money

- Child labour
- TV viewing
- Smoking
- Drinking
- Drugs
- Juvenile Crime

Infant mortality

Table 9 presents data for the UK on the mortality rates of children for selected years since 1961 and for the 1980s. It can be seen that all these vital statistics have shown a continuing decline during the 1980s.

Table 9: Vital statistics : UK Rates per 1,000

	Infant mortality rate	Neonatal mortality rate	Still birth rate	Perinatal mortality rate
1961	22.1	15.8	19.3	32.7
1966	19.6	13.2	15.5	26.7
1971	17.9	12.0	12.6	22.6
1976	14.5	9.9	9.7	18.0
1981	11.2	6.7	6.6	12.0
1983	10.2	5.9	5.8	10.5
1984	9.6	5.7	5.7	10.2
1985	9.4	5.4	5.5	9.9
1986	9.5	5.3	5.3	9.6
1987	9.1	5.0	5.0	9.0
1988	9.0	4.9	4.9	8.8
1989	8.4	4.7	4.9	8.3

Source: *Population Trends 61*

However the decline in infant mortality rates has been much slower in the 1980s than in previous decades (Social Services Committee: 1988b). It is arguable that infant mortality becomes harder to reduce beyond a certain level. However rates in the UK have declined more slowly than in some other countries and are still high in comparison with for example, France 7.9 (1986), Italy 8.1 (1985) and Sweden 5.9 (1986) (National Children's Home [NCH]: 1989). Had the infant mortality rate in England and Wales been that of Sweden in 1986, 2,247 children would not have died (figures derived from Department of Health (DOH): 1990 and *Population Trends*). England and Wales had the highest postneonatal mortality rate of seven selected western countries studied by Kleinman and Kieley (1990). The only group having a higher rate was that of US Blacks. There are sharp regional differences in infant mortality rates – in 1987 they varied from 7.8 in East Anglia to 9.9 in Yorkshire and Humberside. There has been considerable debate about whether differentials in infant mortality between social classes in Britain have diminished (Carr Hill:1988, Townsend and Davidson: 1982, Illsley and Le Grand: 1987). From the end of the 1940s to the early 1970s there was a widening differential in infant mortality rates between the unskilled social classes and the rest. It was thought that this gap narrowed in the late 1970s (Townsend and Davidson: 1982), however, a subsequent analysis revealed that social class data of children born outside marriage had been excluded. It is difficult to draw firm conclusions about recent trends until data on the later 1980s have been analysed with regard to such children (Davey-Smith et al: 1990). Nevertheless infant mortality rates in social class V are still double those of social class I (NCB: 1987). If the average infant mortality rate of the population of England and Wales had been that of social class I in 1987, there would have been 1,500 fewer infant deaths. Differentials in perinatal mortality have been maintained between 1975 and 1989. Postneonatal mortality rates have remained static since the mid 1970s (Rodrigues and Botting: 1989), however, class differentials have narrowed as rates in the manual classes have continued to fall whilst non-manual class rates have levelled off.

There are large local differences in low birth weight and deaths in infants which are closely related to indicators of social deprivation (Townsend et al:1988). Although infant mortality has decreased, socio-economic related causes of death have shown much less improvement and have become proportionately much larger problems. For example Sudden Infant Death Syndrome has become a major deprivation-related health problem in postneonates accounting for 46 per cent of postneonatal mortality in England and Wales in 1986. Some of the increase in Sudden Infant Death Syndrome (from 1,099 deaths in 1979 to 1,629 deaths in 1988 in England and Wales) might be due to a shift to this classification of deaths previously certified as due to a respiratory cause (Pharoah: 1986). A number of improvements in causes of death such as infections give no cause for complacency and are definitely related to socio-economic deprivation. For example inner city areas have poor levels of immunisation; poor housing and overcrowding; high risks of gastro-enteritis among babies; serious problems of TB among the Asian community; and new infections such as AIDS posing new risks also associated with deprivation. OPCS (1988) has concluded that

'Causes of death which can be regarded as 'preventable'... cause infant deaths in Social Class V at about three times the rate for Social Class I.'

Apart from social class there is an association between infant mortality and low birth weight, and ethnic origin. The percentage of children with low birth weight (less than 2,500 grams) has remained constant at seven per cent for the past 20 years. The downward trend in infant mortality has been due to better intensive care for babies at risk, the changing composition of the population and fewer babies being born in large families and to younger mothers. One offsetting effect has been the increasing proportion of babies born to mothers from the New Commonwealth which now represents eight per cent of total births. The rate of infant deaths in 1986 among women born in Pakistan was 14.8 per 1000 compared with 9.4 among women born in the UK (NCH: 1989).

Deaths in the perinatal period now account for most of infant mortality with prematurity, low birthweight and congenital abnormality being the most significant factors (Goodwin: 1989).

Childhood deaths

The pattern of childhood deaths also shows a continuing downward trend (see Table 10).

For older children and young adults, accidents are now the single largest cause of deaths and motor accidents account for the majority of accidental deaths after age four. Accidents are more common among lower socio-economic groups.

Suicide accounted for 9 per cent of child deaths in 1985. Suicide rates for children aged 10-14 have declined from 1.7 per million in the 1940s to 1.3 per million in the 1980s (McClure 1988). An increase

Table 10: Childhood deaths (England and Wales). Rates per 1000

	Male				Female			
	1-4	5-9	10-14	15-19	1-4	5-9	10-14	15-19
1971	0.76	0.44	0.37	0.90	0.63	0.29	0.24	0.39
1976	0.65	0.34	0.31	0.88	0.46	0.24	0.21	0.35
1981	0.53	0.27	0.29	0.82	0.46	0.19	0.19	0.32
1986	0.44	0.21	0.23	0.71	0.40	0.17	0.17	0.29
1988	0.44	0.23	0.26	0.67	0.39	0.15	0.15	0.30
1989	0.44	0.23	0.22	0.72	0.36	0.16	0.16	0.31

Source: *Population Trends 61*

in the rate for females has been offset by a decline in the rate for males. However Lowy et al (1990) in a local study found the suicide rate of people aged 15-34 increased each year between 1975 and 1987, but this may reflect a shift in Coroners' willingness to record a verdict of suicide. The number of suicides among children aged 10-19 were 128 in 1979 and 134 in 1987 (Mortality Statistics).

Child morbidity

There are no reliable national data on trends in the prevalence of handicapping conditions. The number of abortions due to foetal abnormality have declined over the decade mainly due to a decline in rubella in pregnancy. Nevertheless advances in the prevention and prenatal diagnosis of congenital abnormalities leading to abortion have had an impact in the incidence of some conditions including spina bifida, rubella syndrome, and possibly Down's syndrome. However the main feature of childhood morbidity has been the increasing prevalence of chronically ill and handicapped children in the population. Improved treatment and advances in surgical management have helped to keep disabled children alive longer including children with cystic fibrosis, congenital heart disease and other physical abnormalities.

The first nationally representative estimates of the prevalence of *disability* among children were published by OPCS in 1989 (Bone and Meltzer: 1989). The OPCS survey found that there were 360,000 children with disabilities in Great Britain, with 5,600 of these living in communal establishments. This is a prevalence rate of 32 per 1,000 children. The increased numbers of children surviving with chronic illnesses and handicap are likely to be deprived in relation to their peers because of the increased cost to their families of caring for them (Baldwin:1985). Table 11 shows that there was an increase in the proportion of both boys and girls who were reported by parents as having long-standing illness between 1974 and 1987. There is also evidence from this table that demands on the health care services by children have increased.

Table 11: Trends in the percentage of children with reported morbidity

	Males 1974	Males 1983	Males 1987	Females 1974	Females 1983	Females 1987
Long standing illness						
0– 4	6	11 ⎫	16	5	9 ⎫	13
5–15	10	17 ⎭		7	13 ⎭	
Limiting long standing illness						
0– 4	6	3 ⎫	7	2	2 ⎫	6
5–15	5	8 ⎭		3	6 ⎭	
Restricted activity						
0– 4	10	15 ⎫	13	9	14 ⎫	13
5–15	8	12 ⎭		8	11 ⎭	
Attending outpatients						
0– 4	9	10	12	7	9	11
0–15	8	10	11	6	9	9
Consulting family doctor						
0– 4	14	21	25	15	20	21
5–15	8	10	11	8	9	12
Average number of consultations						
0– 4	5	7	8	5	6	7
5–15	2	3	4	2	3	4

Source: General Household Survey

Admissions of children and young adults (under 19) to *mental illness* hospitals and units have increased from 385 to 417 per 100,000 between 1976 and 1986. Admissions to mental handicap hospitals have increased from 30.2 to 84.8 per 100,000 over the same period (Personal Social Service Statistics: 1989). However, admission statistics are an unreliable indicator of psychiatric morbidity.

Between 1973 and 1983 children's *dental health* improved with a marked decrease in dental decay, particularly among younger children. However half the children entering school still showed signs of dental decay (National Children's Bureau: 1987). Surveys by the British Association for the Study of Community Dentistry indicate no national change in average experience of dental caries between 1983 and 1985/6 for five-year-olds but an accelerated rate of decline in caries in 14-year-olds between 1983 and 1986/7 (DoH: 1990). Carmichael et al (1989) point to the relationship between fluoridation and dental decay in five-year-olds in Newcastle and Northumberland. Their research established that the prevalence of dental decay was related to social class:

'The percentage of subjects with caries experience was substantially higher in Social Classes IV and V than in Social Classes I and II.'

Fluoridation of the water supply was shown to reduce these differentials being most effective (in teeth saved) in social classes (with the highest incidence of dental decay) IV and V. However Carmichael's figures indicate a small rise of dental caries experience between 1981 and 1987 in all categories of the five-year-olds studied.

Although, as we have already seen, there has been an increase in the proportion of children immunised during the 1980s, there have been epidemics of whooping cough in 1982 and 1986 and measles in 1982/83 and 1985/86. *Infectious diseases* account for 10 per cent of all deaths. Notification rates of meningitis in all age groups under 15 are increasing, particularly since 1984. Meningococcal meningitis (accounting for 40 per cent of cases) has risen particularly steeply amongst younger children. AIDS poses a new threat to child health and survival via child sexual abuse, infection *in utero* and, among adolescents, intravenous drug use. By the end of February 1990, 23 children in the UK were reported with AIDS of whom 13 had died (AIDS letter: 1990). In addition there were over 200 children who were known to be HIV positive. There is a particular problem of HIV positive cases among intravenous drug users in Scotland (NCH: 1989). There has been a rise in the notification rates of food poisoning amongst children during the 1980s (DoH: 1990).

Child development

Height: The National Study of Health and Growth (NSHG) has surveyed children aged 4 to 11 since 1972 in England and Scotland. The surveys indicated trends towards taller children from 1972 to 1979 but between 1979 and 1986 this slowed or stopped altogether

(DoH: 1990). Carr Hill (1986) reports evidence from the DES that there is no evidence that the secular trend in growth is continuing at the present time. There is evidence from the survey of the Diets of British School Children (DoH: 1989) that children from families where the father is unemployed or where families are on benefits are significantly shorter. The same study confirmed previous evidence that children from higher social classes are taller than others and Carr Hill (1988) has demonstrated that there has been no discernible diminution in differentials between social classes in heights at age 20 – 24 between 1940 and 1980. The 1983 NSHG was also enhanced to take into separate consideration children from ethnic minorities and inner cities. Afro-Caribbean children were generally taller than all other groups whilst inner city whites and other minority ethnic groups were generally shorter than the 1982 representative sample (DoH: 1990).

Weight: Problems associated with weight appear to be on the increase both in terms of obesity which has increased, and for girls, particularly, anorexia nervosa has been an increasing problem.

'The increasing number of children at the extremes of fatness and thinness reveal new areas of physical health problems with causes that are chiefly behavioural and difficult to manage' (National Children's Bureau: 1987, p.70).

Nutrition: There is anxiety (Whitehead: 1988) that the nutrition of children has deteriorated during the 1980s because of the abolition of price maintenance and the nutritional standards for school meals. The main sources of dietary energy in the diets of British school children are bread, chips, milk, biscuits, meat products, cake and puddings. Higher consumption of chips occurs among lower social classes, children of unemployed fathers and families on benefit. Three-quarters of children have excessive fat intakes. The intake of iron, riboflavin and calcium among girls is below recommended levels and Scottish primary school children are low on vitamin C and beta carotene. School meals when they are eaten contain between 30 and 43 per cent of average daily energy intake and older children, particularly girls, taking food at out of school outlets have the poorest diets (DoH: 1989). Lobstein (1988) estimates the expenditure on food for families on benefit, derived from the Department of Health and Social Security's (DHSS) manual issued to staff, DHSS recommended calorie intakes, and figures from the London Food

Commission detailing the cost of twenty main food items. He found that in terms of total nutrients per day the diets were 'grossly inadequate' with serious deficiencies in the intake of iron, zinc, magnesium, vitamin C and folic acid. Similar results have been obtained by Bradshaw and Holmes (1989) and Bradshaw and Morgan (1987) using different methods.

Racial disadvantage

Between 1984 and 1986 ethnic minorities represented 8.1 per cent of the population aged 1–15 (Haskey:1988). Indian, Pakistani and Caribbean are the largest ethnic groups and represent over half the total. Almost three quarters of the minority ethnic population live in metropolitan counties, concentrated in inner city areas in poor and overcrowded housing conditions. Infant mortality is, as has been seen earlier, much higher in certain ethnic groups than in the rest of the population and ethnic groups have their own special health problems such as sicklecell anaemia and thalassaemia.

Black children in Britain experience disadvantage and deprivation through racism and discrimination that permeates many areas. Their parents are more likely to be unemployed or low paid; their housing is likely to be overcrowded and lacking amenities; access to public services, even access to schools in some areas, is more difficult for them. Afro-Caribbean children and those of mixed parentage are also more likely to be admitted to local authority care than are white or Asian children (Rowe et al: 1989). One contributory factor may be the disproportionately high number of Black women in prison (NACRO: 1989). Black children also encounter additional adjustments whilst growing up in managing the transition from or maintaining their ethnic culture.

Homelessness and housing conditions

Although official statistics do not show the full extent of the crisis of homelessness there is no doubt that it has increased as a problem during the 1980s, and 79 per cent of homeless households in priority need in 1988 included dependent children and/or pregnant women (*Social Trends*: 1990). Table 12 gives the number of homeless households involving children up to 1988.

If the rate of increase continued to the end of the decade the number of homeless households will have doubled since 1981.

Table 12: Number of homeless households involving children

	England and Wales	Great Britain
1981	57,000	–
1985	73,000	–
1986	–	87,360
1987	83,000	92,352
1988	–	96,854

Source: NCH 1989 and 1990

An Association of Metropolitan Authorities (AMA) working party found a dearth of information and research into Black homelessness (1988) but notes that in London

'black households are some three or four times as likely to become statutorily homeless as white households'. (para. 1.7)

There has also been a dramatic increase in the number of young people aged between 16 and 19 who are homeless and often living rough on the streets of large cities. Shelter (1989) (the housing pressure group) estimated that over 150,000 experience homelessness every year as a result of leaving home or care and being unable to find or afford accommodation. These problems have been exacerbated not only by the shortage of housing and hostel accommodation but changes in social security rules that removed entitlement for 16 and 17-year-olds and reduced it for other young people (Craig and Glendinning: 1990a). A third of homeless young people are thought to be in London, however it is also thought to be a growing provincial problem.

Greve and Currie (1990) state there has been a rapid increase in the use of bed and breakfast accommodation to house homeless families with children and concern has been expressed at the impact of this type of accommodation on health, development, safety, education and diet.

'In spite of being a high risk group, hotel children seem to have poor access to health services. Records suggest that they tend to miss developmental checks, immunisation and vaccination.' (Conway: 1988 p.76)

'A high proportion of families being placed in bed and breakfast hotels are black: Tower Hamlets for example, has informed a House of Commons Committee that 80 per cent of families it houses in hotels are of Bengali origin.' (Association of Metropolitan Authorities: 1988)

Family homelessness can also lead to children being placed in care. In 1987 in Great Britain a total of 408 children were in care specifically for this reason. This was a reduction from 1986 but according to NCH (1990)

'The change (decrease) has occurred as a result of a change in policy, and the belief by social workers that homelessness in itself does not constitute grounds for care proceedings.' (p.15)

House price inflation and high interest rates have exacerbated the crisis in homelessness with repossessions by building societies increasing from 4,000 in 1981 to 14,000 in 1989 (*Social Trends*: 1990).

As well as an increase in homelessness there is evidence that housing conditions for families with children have deteriorated between 1981 and 1986. The report of the English House Conditions Survey (Department of Environment: 1988) concluded that

'Single parent families, families with one or two children...were the groups most likely to have experienced some deterioration in their housing conditions. In particular, households with one or two children occupied in 1981 substantially less than their expected share of dwelling which were unfit or in 'serious' disrepair, but by 1986 this position had reversed.' (Para.9.23)

Poor families with children are likely to live in public sector housing in urban areas. A recent survey of a random sample of 579 families with children in Glasgow, Edinburgh and London found that a third of dwellings contained damp and almost half contained mould growth. The study concluded that damp and mouldy housing conditions have adverse effects on symptomatic health particularly among children (Platt et al: 1988).

Disconnections from gas supply due to non payment increased from 35,000 a year in 1979 to 61,000 in 1987 but fell in 1989 to 19,000 due, probably, to changes in disconnection policy. Electricity disconnections fell from 99,000 a year in 1979 to 70,000 a year in 1989 (National Consumer Council: 1990, p.125).

Clothing

There are no data on changes in the adequacy of clothing over time. However Bradshaw and Morgan (1987) have examined expenditure on children's clothing by unemployed families and single parents on benefit and concluded that families cannot maintain minimum clothing stocks with their level of expenditure (see also Craig and Glendinning: 1990b). In a later study Bradshaw and Holmes (1989) compared the clothing stocks of families with an unemployed head with a minimum standard. They found that 60 per cent of children in the sample were below standard on two or more essential items.

Child protection

The number of children in care was reasonably constant between 1974 and 1980 and then fell in the early 1980s. After 1985 the number of children removed to a place of safety increased and so did the rate per 1,000 of the population under 18 but it declined slightly in 1988 (NCH: 1990). In 1981 6,212 children were removed to a place of safety in England or 0.52 per 1,000 and by 1987 this had increased to 8,055 and 0.73 respectively. However since the early 1980s the number of children in the care of the local authorities in England has declined from 88,663 in 1982 to 67,326 in 1986 or from 7.47 per 1,000 to 6.04 per 1,000 (NCH: 1989). There has, over time, been a decline in the proportion of those in care in residential children's homes and an increase in the proportion boarded out with foster carers. In 1987 52 per cent of children in care in England were boarded out.

Child abuse

The issue of physical and sexual child abuse has come to the fore in the 1980s and it is impossible to say whether this is due to heightened awareness of an existing problem or due to growth in its prevalence. Given the nature of the subject, child abuse has been difficult to investigate in terms of its extent and growth. One of the main sources of information since the 1970s has been the National Society for the Prevention of Cruelty to Children (NSPCC) who set up Child Abuse Registers in England and Wales in 1974 and 1975. Between 1977 and 1986 nearly 12,500 children were placed on the NSPCC register as abused or at risk of being abused. The majority of those who had been abused suffered from physical injuries of some kind (81 per cent) with nearly 10 per cent of injuries serious or fatal and 11 per cent of the children were sexually abused (Creighton: 1988). Over the period the proportion of children who were injured fell and the proportion who were sexually abused rose from 3 per cent in 1981 to 32 per cent in 1986. At about the same time as the NSPCC register was established local authorities established Child Protection Registers. In 1989 there were 40,700 children on the registers in England. This was 3.7 per 1000 children under 18 but the rate varied from 7.4 per 1000 in Inner London to 2.1 per 1000 in Thames/Anglia. In 1989 there were 22,000 new registrations (NCH: 1990).

Retrospective surveys of the general population have shown that only a small proportion of abuse is reported; thus it seems probable that these figures are underestimates (La Fontaine: 1990).

Due to differing methodological practices and definitions, studies have produced varying estimates of the incidence of sexual abuse of children. A prevalence study of just over 2000 men and women using a broad definition of sexual abuse found that 10 per cent had some experience of sexual abuse prior to the age of 16 (Baker and Duncan: 1985). Another involving 600 women found that 46 per cent had been abused as children (West: 1985) and in another survey of 1236 women (Hall: 1985) 21 per cent reported such abuse, more than once in a third of cases.

Table 13 provides data on the number of notifiable sexual offences and child homicides in England and Wales. It shows that prosecutions for buggery, incest and gross indecency have all increased during the latter part of the 1980s but there was no increase in homicide.

Table 13: Notifiable sexual offences and homicides of children under 16

	1984	1985	1986	1987	1988
Incest	290	277	444	511	516
Gross indecency with a child	472	633	666	831	871
Unlawful sexual intercourse with girls under 13	270	299	362	312	283
Unlawful sexual intercourse with girls under 16	2622	2733	2555	2699	2552
Buggery	602	633	794	929	951
Homicide under 16	82	103	61	78	N/A

Source: NCH 1990

Educational attainment

Trends in educational inputs have been described earlier. In this section the focus is on attainment. Table 14 shows that the level of educational attainment of both boys and girls has increased between 1975/76 and 1987/88. The overall increase for boys with at least one higher grade GCE O level is from 49 per cent in 1975/76 to 55 per cent in 1987/88.

Table 14: School leavers – highest qualification by sex 1975/76 – 1986/87. Percentages

	Boys		Girls	
	1975/76	1987/88	1975/76	1987/88
2 or more A levels / 3 or more H grades	14	16	12	16
1 A level/1 or more H grades	4	4	4	4
5 or more O levels grades A-C	7	10	10	14
1-4 O level grades A-C	24	24	27	28
1 or more O level grades D or E or CSE grades 2-5	30	32	28	28
No GCE/CSE or CSE grades	21	13	19	9

Source: *Social Trends*

Despite this, recent concern has been expressed regarding Britain's educational performance in comparison to that of other countries. Sir Claus Moser (*Independent* 21 August 1990) recently pointed out that only 35 per cent of British 16 to 18-year-olds were in full time education, whereas figures for the US were 79 per cent, Japan 77 per cent and Sweden 76 per cent.

There are differences in exam performance between ethnic groups – children of Pakistani and Indian origin do better than those of British and Caribbean origin. (ILEA:1990).

Truancy

A recent report (Stoll and O'Keefe: 1989) pointed to a survey of nine secondary schools in which two thirds of all pupils surveyed admitted to truanting, half of whom did so at least once a month. The introduction of the GCSE has apparently worsened the situation, with students now truanting in order to catch up on course work or due to failure to meet a course work deadline, as well as for reasons given as 'boredom or depression'.

Teenage conceptions

It is debatable whether teenage conceptions are really an outcome of poverty and deprivation, nevertheless teenage mothers and their children have a high risk of deprivation. Rates of conception by those under 20 rose from 57.9 per 1000 in 1977 to 66.1 per 1000 in 1987 (England and Wales). The conception rates for girls aged under 16 and aged 16 and 17 also rose (see Table 15).

Table 15: Rates of conceptions among teenagers in England and Wales (per 1000)

Age	1977	1986	1987
Under 14	0.9	0.9	1.1
14	4.9	5.7	5.8
15	17.2	18.5	19.7
16	39.1	41.9	44.1
17	59.1	64.8	67.1
18	78.6	83.6	87.7
19	94.7	93.5	101.1
Total under 20	57.9	62.3	66.1

Source: Birth Statistics (1988)

The percentage of total conceptions leading to legal abortion for girls under 16 rose between 1977 and 1982 from 53 to 57 per cent, however it levelled out in 1986 and 1987 to 54 per cent. For girls under 20 the proportion has continued to rise slowly from 28 per cent in 1977 to 35 per cent in 1987. Thus, overall, the proportion of teenage conceptions leading to births declined from 72 per cent in 1977 to 65 per cent in 1987.

Pocket money

Information from the *Wall's Pocket Money Monitor* (1990) shows that overall pocket money between 1975 and 1990 has risen above the rate of inflation

'If children's pocket money had followed the levels of inflation from 1975, in 1990 they would be receiving £1.19. However, they have done extremely well and on average actually receive 25 per cent above this level.' (p.2)

However further analysis of the figures show that the real increase occurred in the earlier period studied and that the increase since 1982 has been below the rate of inflation.

Child labour

The extent of the child workforce is difficult to assess. The Low Pay Unit (MacLennan et al: 1985, p.15) points out that there are no official information sources on the employment of workers under 16 years, thus most of the data available is derived from local or ad hoc surveys. A local survey carried out by the Low Pay Unit and the Open University (MacLennan et al: 1985) discovered 40 per cent of children surveyed were engaged in 'a trade or occupation carried out for profit' that is, jobs other than babysitting, running errands or other unregulated employment. Examination of a subsample of this data set, although based on a small sample, discovered a relationship between parents' unemployment and the likelihood of children working. The survey discovered approximately 4 out of 5 of the children working in London were employed illegally through either being under age, working in unsuitable jobs or working illegal hours.

TV viewing

The average amount of time spent viewing TV by 4–15-year-olds rose from 16 hours 10 minutes a week in 1984 to 20 hours 35 minutes in 1986, however it has fallen since then to 18 hours 34 minutes in 1988 (*Social Trends*:1990). This follows a general trend showing a decline in TV watching over the late 1980s in the general population. The amount of time spent watching TV increases with age thus the 4–15 age group watched the least TV of the population as a whole.

Smoking

Two national surveys of the smoking habits of secondary school children were carried out in the early 1980s by OPCS. The first survey conducted in 1982 concluded that

'Among all the secondary school children aged 11–16 who took part in the survey, 11 per cent said that they smoked regularly (one or more cigarettes per week) and a further 8 per cent smoked occasionally, but among pupils in their fifth year over a quarter were smoking regularly and a further one in ten occasionally'. (Population Trends: 1985, p.18)

The second survey conducted in 1984 showed small increases in smoking behaviour both for regular and occasional smokers, again the proportion increased with age and by the fifth year nearly a third were regular smokers.

Increasing awareness during the 1980s of the health hazards attached to smoking led to a downturn in the total adult population who smoke. This downturn appears to have been reflected among secondary school children, with the proportion who were regular or occasional smokers falling from 22 per cent in 1984 for girls and boys, to 14 per cent for girls and 12 per cent for boys in 1988 (Dunnell: 1990, fig.9). Unfortunately the number of adult smokers began to rise again in mid-1987 but it is too early to tell how this will be reflected in child smokers and how significant the trend is. The study *Young People in 1988* (Balding 1989a) found that in the four years 1984–88 the number of 14 and 15-year-old boys and 11 and 13-year-old girls who smoke was falling. The General Household Survey (1989) also shows that smoking among 16–19-year-olds fell from 35 per cent to 30 per cent for men and 33 per cent to 30 per cent for women between 1978 and 1986.

Drinking

A very high proportion of teenagers consume alcohol – over three quarters of 13-year-olds in England and Wales were drinking to some extent in 1986. From the age of 15 to 17 the majority of young drinkers obtain their alcohol in pubs which means that a high proportion of children in this age group are involved in under age drinking.

'One out of five 15 year old boys and one out of ten 15 year old girls drink above the recommended safety limits. One in every 14 drunkenness offence is committed by children under the legal age for drinking. Three per cent of 16 year old boys and girls and 9 per cent of 17 year old boys and 4 per cent of 17 year old girls drink almost every day.' (NCH: 1989, p.17)

The Health Education Authority's Education Unit have collected responses to a health related behaviour questionnaire since 1980.

The surveys apparently show little evidence of alcohol consumption increasing or decreasing among the school children questioned (Balding: 1989b).

Drugs

The number of notified drug addicts under the age of 21 has increased considerably through the 1980s from 489 in 1982 to 1443 in 1989 (NCH: 1990). These official figures are only the tip of the iceberg of drug abuse as only a minority of actual drug abusers register with the appropriate authorities and appear as notified addicts.

Solvent abuse has been a particular and growing problem among children. The issue of solvent abuse first came to light in Scotland in 1970. By 1975 estimates for the Glasgow area suggest that over 2000 young people were involved in solvent abuse. Studies conducted in Scotland also suggest that the age at which children are being affected by this problem is becoming progressively lower and at the moment most abusers are aged between 10 and 15. O'Connor (1986) suggests that between 3 and 5 per cent of 15-year-olds have used solvents and that 10 per cent of this group will develop a chronic abuse problem. The NCH (1989) reported that more pupils use solvents daily than any other single drug. The average age at which solvents are first used is below 13 and there is a rising trend of solvent abuse among girls.

Trends in deaths associated with abuse of volatile substances have been monitored at St George's Hospital Medical School (Anderson et al: 1990). The annual number of UK deaths rose from 17 in 1978 to 134 in 1988. Mortality was higher amongst males than females in both age categories 10 to 14 and 15 to 19. The age/sex category showing the highest mortality rate (29 per million in 1988) was 15 to 19-year-old males and the lowest, 10 – 14-year-old females (2 per million in 1988); however, mortality rates in all age/sex categories appear to be rising.

Trends in different types of substances associated with death show an increase – aerosol death (from 13 to 46 a year), and gas fuel deaths (from 19 to 53 a year) between 1983 and 1988, whilst numbers of glue deaths have overall decreased slightly from 24 in 1983 to 16 in 1988.

Juvenile Crime

Criminal statistics are notoriously affected by the behaviour of the police and the courts. Over time offences are reclassified, there are changes in police recording and variations in detection rates, all of which undermine the reliability of statistics on crime. Young Blacks have been shown to be particularly vulnerable to discrimination in the criminal justice system. In Willis' 1983 study, young Black males were stopped by police approximately ten times more often than average, whilst Landau and Nathan (1983) discovered that white juveniles had a much greater chance of being cautioned (as opposed to charged) than Black juveniles.

In England and Wales the number of juveniles aged 10–16 years sentenced or cautioned for indictable offences fell from 164,000 in 1979 to 119,000 in 1988, a fall of 27 per cent. Part of this fall can be accounted for by the decrease in the population aged 10–16 years. However there has also been a decline in the rate of young persons cautioned or sentenced in the second half of the 1980s. The number per 100 rose from 2.9 in 1979 to 3.6 in 1985 and fell back to 3.0 in 1987. There has been an increase in the use of cautions which might have been expected to have led to net widening consequences particularly given the increase in police numbers (Pratt: 1985). The rates at which young people have been found guilty and sentenced for indictable offences has declined from 1.45 per 100 in 1979 to 0.92 in 1987. There has been very little change in the type of offences committed by juveniles during the decade – over two thirds involve theft and the handling of stolen property. In the 14–16 age range the percentage of males sentenced to custody remained constant at 11 per cent whilst that for females has risen slightly from 1 – 2 per cent.

There has been a rise in the number of young adult offenders aged 17 – 20 of 18 per cent between 1979 and 1987 and the rate of offenders has also risen from 3.6 per 100 to 4.1 per 100. Despite these trends just over a quarter of all offenders in 1986 were juveniles. Delinquency has been associated with long term unemployment, family breakdown and poverty (Graham: 1989, Tarling: 1982). All of these have increased in the 1980s.

8. Conclusions

During the 1980s children have borne the brunt of the changes that have occurred in the economic conditions, demographic structure and social policies of the UK. More children have been living in low income families and the number of children living in poverty has doubled. Inequalities have also become wider. There is no evidence that improvements in the living standards of the better off have 'trickled down' to low income families with children.

What have been the results of this increase in child poverty and deprivation? Here the conclusions are more tentative because the evidence is not very good, the impacts have probably yet to be observed and the manner in which social and economic change affects the lives of children is not well understood. An array of outcomes has been considered in this review and the picture that emerges is mixed. For some indicators of outcome we just do not know whether things have got worse – for example child abuse and child sexual abuse. Some indicators suggest that things have got better – educational attainment, teenage crime, smoking in childhood and adolescence all show improvements. Some indicators also show improvement but perhaps at a slower rate than in previous periods or at a slower rate that might be expected in comparison with other countries – for example infant mortality. Finally there are those indicators that more clearly suggest things have got worse – homelessness, housing conditions, childhood morbidity, drug abuse and probably also children's diets.

This overall picture hides great variation in outcome. Inequalities in children's lives have increased. The lives of children in a two parent, two earner family, living in owner occupied housing, in the south of England, served by good public services have improved. In contrast the lives of children in an unemployed or lone parent family, living in rented accommodation, in the inner city with deteriorating health, education and social services have got worse. Black children and families are particularly disadvantaged on many fronts.

There is a danger that after all this, recommendations for policy will appear facile. It is obvious for example that a key determinant of children's lives is the state of the economy and the access of their parents to employment for decent wages. A child centred economic policy is one that gives priority to reducing unemployment. The living standards of children will also be enhanced by policies that make it easier for families (women) to combine work and child care responsibilities. The incomes of families with children need to be enhanced through child centred social security and fiscal policies. Here a debate immediately opens up about whether the best approach is through universal child benefits, selective income related benefits, the reintroduction of child tax allowances or a combination of all three. However any of these strategies would help to reverse the increase in inequalities between families with children and childless people that has taken place over the last decade. Beyond these policies it is to maintaining and improving services that we must look to protect children's health and well being.

Perhaps the most important conclusion to be drawn from this review is that there is a need to develop better mechanisms than we have for monitoring the state of children in the UK. The impact of social and economic change on children is important enough for there to be an *Annual Report on The State of Children in the UK*. The National Children's Homes Factfile produced annually on *Children in Danger* is an approach to this; so is the National Children's Bureau (1987) report on child health, *Investing in the Future*. Also it is to be welcomed, that with the help of OPCS, the Central Health Monitoring Unit in the Department of Health has begun to draw together the wide variety of information available on child health (Dunnell: 1990) but the effort needs to be broadened to other aspects of children's lives. Finally in order to monitor the lives of children properly, new information will need to be collected. In particular we need to know more about what children themselves think and feel.

References

Abel Smith, B. and Townsend, P., *The Poor and the Poorest*. Occasional papers on social administration No.17: G Bell and Sons Ltd: 1965.

AIDS letter, 17 February/March, p.2: 1990.

Anderson, H.R., Ramsey, J.D. and Bloor, K., *Trends in deaths associated with abuse of volatile substances 1971–88*. St George's Hospital Medical School, Report No.3: June 1990.

Association of Metropolitan Authorities, *A Strategy for Racial Equality in Housing, a policy and good practice guide for local authorities*. No.2, Homelessness: report of local authority housing and racial equality working party. June 1990.

Atkinson A. B. and Micklewright J., Turning the Screw: Benefits for the Unemployed 1979–88 *in* Dilnot A. and Walker I. (eds) *The Economics of Social Security*. Oxford University Press: 1989.

Baker, A. and Duncan, S., Child Sexual Abuse: a study of prevalence in Great Britain, *Child Abuse and Neglect*, Vol.9, no.4: 1985.

Balding, J., *Young People in 1988*. Health Education Authority Schools Education Unit: University of Exeter: 1989a.

Balding, J., *The HEA Survey on Alcohol use among school children*. Paper presented to the Conference, Alcohol, Young People and Health Education, Institute of Alcohol Studies: London: July 1989b.

Baldwin, S., *The Costs of Caring*. Routledge and Kegan Paul: 1985.

REFERENCES

Bone, M. and Meltzer, H., *The Prevalence of Disability Among Children*. HMSO: 1989.

Bradshaw, J. and Morgan, J., *Budgeting on Benefit*. Family Policy Studies Centre: 1987.

Bradshaw, J. and Piachaud, D., *Child Support in the European Community*. Bedford Square Press: 1980.

Bradshaw, J. and Holmes, H., *Living on the Edge: a study of the living standards of families on benefit in Tyne and Wear*. Tyneside Child Poverty Action Group: 1989.

Carmichael, C.L., Rugg-Gunn, A.J. and Ferrell, R.S., The Relationship between Fluoridation, Social Class and Caries Experience in 5-year-old children in Newcastle and Northumberland in 1987, *British Dental Journal*, Vol.167, No.2, pp.57–61, 22 July: 1989.

Carr Hill, R., *Trends in Health, Mimeo*: 1986.

Carr Hill, R., Time Trends in Inequality in Health, *J. Biosoc. Sci.*, No. 20, pp.265–273: 1988.

Central Statistical Office, *Economic Trends*, No. 422, December, HMSO: 1988.

Central Statistical Office, *Economic Trends*, No. 439, May, HMSO: 1990.

Central Statistical Office, *Regional Trends*, No. 25, HMSO: 1990.

Central Statistical Office, *Social Trends*, No. 19, HMSO: 1989.

Central Statistical Office, *Social Trends*, No. 20, HMSO: 1990.

Child Poverty Action Group, *Facts and Figures*, Poverty Pamphlet No. 74. CPAG: 1989.

Children Act 1989.

Clarke, L., *Children's Changing Circumstances: recent trends and future prospects*. University of London, Centre for Population Studies: 1989.

Conway, J. (ed), *Prescription for Poor Health*. Shelter: 1988.

Craig, G. and Glendinning, C., *The Impact of Social Security Changes: the views of young people*. Barnardo's, Research and Development Section. Unpublished: 1990a.

Craig, G. and Glendinning, C., *The Impact of Social Security Changes: the views of families using Barnardo's pre-school services.* Barnardo's, Research and Development Section: 1990b.

Creighton, S.J., The Incidence of Child Abuse and Neglect, in Browne, K, Davies, C. and Stratton, P. (eds) *Early Prediction and Prevention of Child Abuse.* Wiley: 1988.

Davey-Smith, G., Bartley, M. and Blane, D., The Black Report on socioeconomic inequalities in health 10 years on, *British Medical Journal*, Vol.301, 18–25 August, pp.373–377: 1990.

Department of Employment, 'Labour Force Outlook in the Year 2000', *Employment Gazette.* April, pp.159–172: 1989.

Department of Environment, *English House Conditions Survey 1986.* HMSO: 1988.

Department of Health, *Diets of British School Children.* HMSO: 1989.

Department of Health, *An Epidemiological Overview of Child Health.* Unpublished: 1990.

Department of Health, *Health and Personal Social Services Statistics for England, 1989.* HMSO: 1989.

Department of Health and Social Security, *Households Below Average Income: A Statistical Analysis 1981–85.* DHSS: 1988.

Department of Social Security, *Abstract of Statistics for Index of Retail Prices, Average Earnings and Social Security Benefits and Contributions.* DSS: 1989.

Department of Social Security, *Households below Average Income: A Statistical Analysis 1981–1987.* Government Statistical Service: 1990.

Department of Social Security, *Social Security Statistics 1989.* HMSO: 1990

Dunnell, K., Monitoring children's health, *Population Trends*, No. 60, pp.16–22: 1990.

Education (No. 2) Act 1986.

Freeman, M.D.A., Taking Children's Rights Seriously, *Children and Society*, Vol.1, No.4, pp.299–319: 1987–88.

REFERENCES

General Household Survey, OPCS, HMSO: 1989.

Gillick v West Norfolk and Wisbech Area Health Authority, 1 FLR, No. 1,p.224: 1986.

Goodwin, S., *Health for all Children: Preventive Child Health*. Paper given at NCB/NAHA Conference, 6 December, Kensington Town Hall: 1989.

Graham, J., Families, Parenting Skills and Delinquency. *Home Office Research Bulletin* No. 26: 1989.

Greve, J. and Currie, E., Homeless in Britain, *Housing Research Findings*, No.10, February. Joseph Rowntree Memorial Trust: 1990.

Hall, R., *Ask Any Woman*. Falling Wall Press: 1985.

Halsey, A.H. (ed), *British Social Trends since 1900: a guide to the changing social structure of Britain*. Macmillan: 1988.

Hansard, 8 May 1989, col.332.
Hansard, 6 November 1989, col.459.
Hansard, 20 March 1990, col.518.
Hansard, 1 May 1990, col.491.
Hansard, 5 May 1990, col.98.
Hansard, 22 May 1990, col.98.

Haskey, J., The Ethnic Minority Population of Great Britain: their size and characteristics, *Population Trends*, No. 54. HMSO: 1988.

Haskey, J., One Parent Families and their Children in Great Britain: numbers and their characteristics, *Population Trends*, No. 55. HMSO: 1989.

Haskey, J. and Kiernan, K., Cohabitation in Great Britain – characteristics and estimated numbers of cohabiting partners, *Population Trends*, No. 58. HMSO: 1989.

Hill, J., *Changing Tax: how the tax system works and how to change it*. CPAG: 1989.

HM Treasury, *Autumn Statement 1989*. Cm.879, HMSO: 1989.

Illsley, R. and Le Grand, J., The Measurement of Inequality in Health, *in* Williams, A. (ed) *Health and Economics*. Macmillan: 1987.

Inner London Education Authority, *Differences in Examination Performance, Report of Strategic Policy Sub-committee of the Education Committee*. 7 March 1990, No.19086 ILEA.

Institute for Fiscal Studies, Low Income Families 1979-1987. *mimeo*: 1990.

Johnson, P. and Stark, G., *Taxation and Social Security 1979–1989: the report on household incomes*. Institute for Fiscal Studies: 1989.

Kiernan, K. and Wicks, M., *Family Change and Future Policy*. Joseph Rowntree Memorial Trust and Family Policy Studies Centre: 1990.

Kleinman, J.C. and Kieley, J.L., *Postneonatal Mortality in the United States: an international perspective*. National Centre for Health Statistics, Hyattsville, USA. Unpublished: 1990.

La Fontaine, J., *Child Sexual Abuse*. Polity: 1990.

Le Grand, J., *The Strategy of Equality: redistribution and the social services*. Allen and Unwin: 1982.

Lobstein, T., Poor Children and Cheap Calories, *Community Paediatric Group Newsletter*, Autumn, p.4: 1988.

Landau and Nathan, Discrimination in the Criminal Justice System, *British Journal of Criminology*, Vol.23, April: 1983.

Low Pay Unit, *Ten Years On: The Poor Decade*. Low Pay Unit: 1989.

Low Pay Unit, Scrapping Minimum Wages in Britain; will it mean more pay cuts for the poor, *Parliamentary Briefing*, 8 March: 1990.

Lowy, A., Burton, P. and Briggs, A., Increasing suicide rates in young adults, *British Medical Journal*, Vol.300, p.643, 10 March: 1990.

MacLennan, E., Fitz, J. and Sullivan, J., *Working Children*. Low Pay Pamphlet No.34, Low Pay Unit: 1985.

McClure, G.M.G., Suicide in England and Wales, *Journal of Child Psychology and Psychiatry*, Vol. 29, No.3, pp. 345–9: 1988.

Millar, J., *Poverty and the Lone-Parent Family: The Challenge to Social Policy*. Avebury: 1989.

NACRO, *Some Facts and Findings about Black People in the Criminal Justice System*. NACRO Briefing, May: 1989.

National Childcare Campaign/Daycare Trust, *Under five and under funded*. National Childcare Campaign/Daycare Trust: 1984.

National Children's Bureau, *Investing in the Future: child health ten years after the Court Report*. NCB: 1987.

National Children's Home, *Children in Danger: NCH Factfile about Children Today*. NCH: 1989.

National Children's Home, *Children in Danger: NCH Factfile about Children Today*. NCH: 1990.

National Consumer Council, *Credit and Debt*. NCC: 1990.

O'Connor, D.J., *Glue Sniffing and Solvent Abuse*. Boys and Girls Welfare Society: 1986.

OPCS, *Birth Statistics 1988*. HMSO: 1990.

OPCS, *Mortality Statistics: Cause 1987*. Series DH2. HMSO: 1989.

OPCS, *Occupational Mortality 1979–1980 and 1982–83*. Childhood Supplement series D5 no 8 para 2–3–2, HMSO *vide* Social Services Committee 1988b para 43: 1988.

OPCS, *Population Trends*, Smoking Among Secondary School Children. No. 42, HMSO: 1985.

OPCS, *Population Trends*, Vital Statistics. No. 61, HMSO: 1990.

Pharoah, P.O.D., Perspectives and Patterns, *British Medical Bulletin*, Vol.42, no.2, pp.119–126: 1986.

Platt, D. et al, Damp Housing, Mould Growth and Symptomatic Health States, *British Medical Journal*, Vol. 298, 1673: 1988.

Pratt, J., Delinquency as a Scarce Resource, *The Howard Journal*, Vol. 24, No. 2, pp.93–107: 1985.

Roll, J., Measuring Family Income: A Recent Controversy in the Use of Official Statistics, *Social Policy and Administration*, Vol. 22, No. 2, pp.134–149: 1988.

Rodrigues, L. and Botting, B., Recent trends in postneonatal mortality in England, *Population Trends* 55. pp.7–15: 1989.

Rowe, J. et al, *Child Care Now*. Batsford: 1989.

Shelter, taken from Gosling, J. and Diarists, *One day I'll have a place of my own*, p.29 Central London Social Security Advisors' Forum and Shelter: London: 1989.

Social Services Committee, *Families on Low Income: Low Income Statistics*. Fourth Report, Session 1987–88, HC 565, HMSO: 1988a

Social Services Committee, *Perinatal, Neonatal and Infant Mortality*. First Report, Session 1988–89, HC 54, HMSO: 1988b.

Social Services Committee, *Social Security: Changes Implemented in April 1988*. Ninth Report, HC 437, HMSO: 1989a.

Social Services Committee, *Resourcing the National Health Service: The Government's plans for the future of the National Health Service*. Eighth Report session 1988–89, 19 July HMSO: 1989b.

Social Trends: see Central Statistical Office

Stoll, P. and O'Keefe, D., *Officially Present*. Institute of Economic Affairs: 1989.

Tarling, R., Unemployment and Crime, *Home Office Research Bulletin*, No. 14: 1982.

Townsend, P. and Davidson, M., *Inequalities in Health: The Black Report*. Penguin: 1982.

Townsend, P., Phillimore, P. and Beattie, A., *Health and Deprivation: Inequality in the North*. Croom Helm: 1988.

Unemployment Unit, *Working Brief*. Unemployment Unit and Youthaid: 1990.

UNICEF, *The State of the World's Children*. Oxford University Press: 1989.

Wall's Pocket Money Monitor. Birds Eye Walls Ltd: 1990.

West, D.J., *Sexual Victimisation*. New York, Gower: 1985.

Whitehead, M., *The Health Divide*. Penguin: 1988.

Wicks, M., Family Trends, Insecurities and Social Policy, *Children and Society*, Vol. 3, No. 1, pp.67–80: 1989.

Willis, C.F., *The Use Effectiveness and Impact of Police Stop and Search powers*. Home Office Research Unit, April: 1983.

Index

A
abortion 21, 29, 36, 46
accidental death 36
  see also death
Afro-Caribbean people 39, 40
  see also Black people
ageing population 23, 28
AIDS 35, 38
  see also infectious diseases
alcohol 48-9
Annual Report on the State of Children in the UK 52
Asian people 35, 40, 41
  see also minority ethnic groups
Auto-Immune Deficiency Syndrome (AIDS) 35, 38
  see also infectious diseases

B
bed and breakfast accommodation 41
  see also homelessness
benefits *see* social security benefits
Bengali people 41
  see also Asian people
Beveridge, William 6
birth cohort studies 4
birth control 21, 30
birth rate
  1945-79: 7-8, 19-20
  1980s: 21-2
  see also conceptions among teenagers; demographic change; maternity services
Black people
  criminal justice system 50
  disadvantage 40, 52
  growth 39
  homelessness 41
  infant mortality 34
  see also minority ethnic groups
'Butskellism' 8

C
capital
  children as human 3
  income from 18
  taxation of 23-4
Care, local authority, children in
  homelessness 41-2
  minority ethnic groups in 40
  reform of policy 29, 43
Caribbean people 39, 40
  see also Black people
caries, dental 38
child abuse 43-4, 51
  see also child protection
child benefit 23-4
child development 38-40
child health services 4, 28-9, 36-8
child labour 47
child protection 29, 40-42, 43
  see also child abuse; Care, local authority
child rearing costs 21, 36
childhood deaths 7, 35-6
  see also infant mortality
childlessness 18, 52
childminders 27
Children Act, 1989: 29-30
children's rights 29-31
children's views 52
clothing 16, 42-3
cohabitation 21
community charge 25
conceptions among teenagers 46
congenital abnormality *see* disabled people
contraception 21, 30
Cornia, Dr. Andrea 1-2
costs of child rearing 21, 36
courts 29-30
crime
  against children 44
  of children and young people 50, 51
cultural adjustment 40
cultural deprivation 16, 40
cystic fibrosis 36

INDEX

D
data on children *see* statistical data
day care 26-7
death in childhood 7, 35-6
　see also demographic change; infant mortality
debt 26
delinquency 50
demographic change 4, 21-2, 23, 27, 28
　see also birth rate; death; family structure; migration
dental health 37-8
　see also health
development, child 38-40
diet 16, 39-40, 51
diphtheria 29
　see also infectious diseases
disabled people
　birth and survival 28-9, 36-8
　in poverty 7, 13-15
　see also health
divorce 21
Down's syndrome 36
　see also learning difficulties
drinking 48-9
drugs 38, 49, 51
dual-earner families 6, 12, 18, 51

E
earnings *see* incomes
economic policies
　1945-1960: 6-7
　1980s: 19-20, 22-31
　recommendations for 52
economic trends 19-21, 23
education
　1945-79: 6,7
　1980s: 26-8, 30-31
　attainment in 45, 51
　spending on, in calculation of income shares 17-18
　see also schools
Education (No. 2) Act, 1986: 30
Education Reform Act, 1988: 30
employment
　1945-79: 6-7
　1980s: 18, 19
　changes in labour markets 1
　fails to overcome poverty 12-15
　low-paid 20-1
　occupational provision to meet need 9
　of children 47
　see also unemployment
environmental conditions 1
ethnic groups *see* minority ethnic groups
European countries
　birth rates 21
　child benefit 23-4
　'decency threshold' for wages 20-21
　education 26-7, 45
　infant mortality 33-4

pre-school provison 27
UNICEF study of 1
examination success 45
expenditure *see* public expenditure

F
family allowances 6
　see also social security benefits
family credit 24
　see also social security benefits
family income supplement 15
　see also social security benefits
family structure
　breakdown of, and juvenile crime 50
　changes in 1, 6-7, 22
　traditional, as social provider 3, 9
　see also demographic change; lone parents
fertility *see* birth rate; conception among teenages
fluoridation of water 38
food *see* diet
foster care 43
　see also Care, local authority
France 33
　see also European countries
fuel disconnections 42
further education 27, 31
　see also education

G
GDP 6,7
Gillick case 30
girls
　alcohol 48
　anorexia nervosa 39
　conception 46
　contraceptive advice 30
　crime 50
　death rate 35
　drugs 49
　educational attainment 45
　growth 38-9
　ill-health 37
　rubella immunisations 29
　sexual abuse of 44
　smoking 48
　suicide 36
　see also women; young people
GNP 23
Gross Domestic product 6,7
Gross National Product 23
growth 38-9
Guardians *ad litem* 30

H
health
　1945-79: 6-7
　1980s: 28-9, 36-8
　housing and 42
　in inner cities 35

minority ethnic groups 35, 40
new statistics on 52
poverty and 4, 13-15
spending on, in calculation of income shares 17-18
Health Education Authority 48-9
health services *see* child health services; maternity services
height 4, 38-9
higher education 28, 31
see also education
HIV 38
homelessness 26, 40-42, 51
see also housing
homicide 44
housing
1945-79: 9
1980s: 24, 26, 40-42, 51
in inner cities 35
spending on, in calculation of income shares 17-18
housing benefit 24
Human Immunodeficiency Virus 38
see also infectious diseases
Hungary 1
see also European countries

I
illegitimacy 22
ill-health *see* health
immunisation 29, 35, 38
impacts on children's well-being 4, 32-50
incest 44
income-related benefits 23-5, 52
see also social security benefits
income support 24-25
see also social security benefits
incomes
1954-76: 6-7
1980s: 17-18, 20, 23
compared with benefits 10-16
Indian people 40
see also minority ethnic groups
infant mortality 4, 7, 33-5, 51
see also death
infectious diseases 29, 35, 38
see also health
inflation 19-20, 23
see also economic policies; prices
inner-city areas 35, 39-41, 44, 52
inputs to children's well-being 4, 6-9, 19-31
Institute of Fiscal Studies 14
insurance, national 6, 23-4
interest
income from 17
high rate of, 1980s: 20, 26, 42
International Year of the Child 29
investment 9, 17, 19, 23
Italy 1, 33
see also European countries

J, K
Japan 1, 45
Keynes, John Maynard 6

L
labour *see* employment
learning difficulties, people with 29, 36, 37
see also disabled people
legal proceedings 29-30
leisure 16
life expectancy 7, 33-6
lone parents
fewer in work 22, 25
in poverty 7, 13-15, 22
increasing numbers 22, 24
social security reforms of 1980s: 25, 52
see also family structure

M
marriage 21, 22
maternity services 4, 28-9
see also birth rate
means-tested benefits 23-5, 52
see also social security benefits
measles 29
see also infectious diseases
meningitis 38
see also infectious diseases
mental health 29, 37
see also health
mentally-handicapped people 29, 36-7
see also disabled people
migration 1
see also demographic change
minority ethnic groups
disadvantaged 40
educational attainment 45
growth 39
low birth weight and infant mortality 35
see also Asian people; Black people
money, children's 46-7
Moore, John 10
morbidity 36-8, 51
see also disabled people
murder 44

N
national assistance 6
see also social security benefits
National Children's Bureau *Preface*, 1, 2, 52
National Children's Homes Factfile 52
national insurance 6, 23-24
see also health; unemployment
National Society for the Prevention of Cruelty to Children 43-4
National Study of Health and Growth 38-9
neonatal mortality 33-5
see also infant mortality
nursery education 26-7
see also education
nutrition 39-40, 51

INDEX

O
one-parent families *see* lone parents
OPCS Survey of Disability in Children 36
outputs to children's well-being 4, 6-9, 19-31
overcrowded housing *see* housing

P,Q
Pakistani people 35, 40
  see also minority ethnic groups
parents
  birth rate 7-8, 21-2
  receiving benefits 10-16, 23-5, 52
  rights and responsibilities 3, 9, 30-31
  see also conceptions among teenagers; lone parents; social security benefits
perinatal mortality 33-4
  see also infant mortality
personal social services 28-9
  see also Care, local authority
playgrounds 4
pocket money 46-7
policies, economic and social
  1945-79: 6-7
  1980s: 19-20, 22-31
  for children's well-being 4
  recommendations for 52
poliomyelitis 29
  see also infectious diseases
population 8
  see also birth rate; death
Portugal 1
  see also European countries
poverty
  1945-79: 6-9
  1980s: 10-16, 17-18, 19-31
  impact of, on children's well-being 32-50
  problem of establishing standard of 10-15
pregnancy, teenage 46
pre-school provision 26-27
  see also schools
prices
  and benefits 16, 23
  of food 39
  of houses 26, 42
  see also inflation
primary education *see* schools
productivity 19-20
protection, child 29, 40, 41-2, 43
  see also child abuse
public expenditure
  1945-79: 7, 9
  1980s: 22-3, 25-9
  in calculation of income shares 17-18
  on children's services 4, 52

R
racial disadvantage 40
  see also minority ethnic groups
rates, local government 25
recreation 16

regional variations
  child abuse 44
  dental health 38
  diet 39
  health funding 28
  HIV 38
  immunisation rates 29
  infant mortality 34
  nursery education 26
rights of children 29-31
rubella 29, 36
  see also disabled people

S
schools
  1945-79: 7, 9, 26
  1980s: 26-8, 30-1
  attainment 4, 45, 51
  governors 30
  meals 28, 39
  students' rights 30-31
  truancy 45-6
  see also education
Scotland 38, 39
secondary education *see* schools
services *see* education; health; housing; personal social services
sexual abuse of children 38, 43-4, 51
  see also child protection
single parents *see* lone parents
slum clearance 9
  see also housing
smoking 47-8, 51
social class inequality
  dental health 38
  growth 39
  income distribution 9, 17-18, 20
  infant mortality 34-5
  taxation 23
social fund 25
  see also social security benefits
social policy *see* policies
social security benefits
  1945-79: 6-7
  1980s: 4, 15-16, 18, 23-5
  and child development 4, 39
  compared with earnings 10-16
  in calculation of income shares 17-18
  recommendations for 52
  young people lose entitlement 25, 31, 41
social services *see* education; housing; personal social services
solvent abuse 49
spending, public *see* public expenditure
spina bifida 36
  see also disabled people
statistical data
  changes in unemployment statistics 20
  debate on validity 10

inadequate 3-4, 14-15, 52
suspension of series 10, 14
stillbirths 33
see also infant mortality
Sudden Infant Death syndrome 34
suicide 36
supplementary benefit
  as measure of poverty 10-16
  replaced by income support 24-5
  see also social security benefits
Sweden, 1, 33-4, 45
  see also European countries

T
taxation
  1945-79: 6-7, 9
  1980s: 22-3, 26
  in calculation of income shares 17-18
  recommendations for 52
teachers 28
  see also schools
television viewing 47
tertiary education 28, 31
  see also education
tetanus 29
  see also infectious diseases
Thatcher, Mrs. Margaret 3, 9
  policies *see* policies
trade, international 19-20
trade disputes 19
truancy 45-6

U
UN Convention on the Rights of the Child 30
under fives 26-7
  see also education
unemployment
  1945-79: 6
  1980s: 13-15, 19-20, 24
  and child development 39
  and juvenile crime 50
  and working children 47
  of young people 27
  recommendations on 52
  see also employment
UNICEF 1-2
Union of Soviet Socialist Republics 1
  see also European countries
United Nations
  Children's Fund 1-2
  Convention on the Rights of the Child 30

United States of America 1, 34, 45
unmarried mothers *see* lone parents; marriage
USA 1, 34, 45
USSR 1
  see also European countries

V
vaccination 29, 35, 38
vital statistics *see* birth rate; death; infant mortality
vitamins 39-40
volatile substance abuse 49
voluntary services 9
vulnerability of children 5

W
wages *see* incomes
Wages Councils 20
wealth, redistribution of 6-9, 17-18
weight 4, 39
'welfare state' 6-9, 23
well-being of children 3-5
  impacts 4, 32-50
  inputs 4, 6-9, 19-31
  outputs 4, 6-9, 19-31
whooping cough 29
  see also infectious diseases
widows 6, 22
women
  as lone parents 21-22
  attitudes to gender roles 21
  earnings 20
  employment 6, 19, 21-2, 52
  in prison 40
  sexually abused 44
  see also girls
work *see* employment
World Summit on Children, 1990: 1

XYZ
young offenders 50
young people
  conception among teenagers 46
  crime 50
  drugs 38, 47-9
  education and training 27-8, 30-31
  employment 19-20
  homelessness 41
  lose right to benefits 25, 31, 41
  unemployment 27
Youth Training Scheme 27